PATHWAYS
TO
REALITY

Erickson-Inspired
Treatment Approaches
to Chemical Dependency

PATHWAYS
TO
REALITY

Erickson-Inspired
Treatment Approaches
to Chemical Dependency

JOHN D. LOVERN, PH.D.

BRUNNER/MAZEL, *Publishers* • NEW YORK

Library of Congress Cataloging-in-Publication Data
Lovern, John D.
    Pathways to reality : Erickson-inspired treatment approaches to
chemical dependency / John D. Lovern.
        p.   cm.
    Includes bibliographical references and index.
    ISBN 0-87630-633-4
    1. Substance abuse—Treatment.   2. Alcoholism—Treatment.
3. Erickson, Milton H.   4. Group psychotherapy.   I. Title.
    [DNLM: 1. Erickson, Milton H.   2.Psychotherapy—methods.
3. Substance Dependence—therapy.   WM 270 L911p]
RC564.L648   1991
616.86′0651—dc20
DNLM/DLC
for Library of Congress   91-13541
                                                                    CIP

Published by
BRUNNER/MAZEL, INC.
19 Union Square West
New York, New York 10003

Manufactured in the United States of America

10   9   8   7   6   5   4   3   2   1

CONTENTS

v

PATHWAYS
TO
REALITY

*Erickson-Inspired
Treatment Approaches
to Chemical Dependency*

1

Introduction

This book is an attempt to share some lessons I learned while applying Milton H. Erickson's ideas in the treatment of my chemically dependent patients. I hope that my efforts here will make a beginning at building a bridge between the addiction treatment community and the growing number of psychotherapists who are utilizing Erickson's teachings in their work. For far too long, most members of the addiction treatment community have remained unaware of the many ways that Erickson's pioneering work can benefit them and their clients and patients. Meanwhile, Erickson-influenced therapists appear to have shied away from the field of addiction treatment.

The apparent reasons for the limited awareness and use of Erickson's ideas and techniques by chemical dependency counselors and therapists include: first, the fact that many treatment people are nonprofessionally trained persons who haven't had broad exposure to schools or theories of psychotherapy; second, addiction treatment people are tied more closely to the philosophy of Alcoholics Anonymous than to any other approach; third, they often distrust psychotherapists; and fourth, so far no one has introduced them to Erickson's ideas or demonstrated the value of these ideas in recovery from addictions.

I hope to show my friends and colleagues in the addiction

treatment field that Milton Erickson has the "right stuff" for them; that his ideas and methods are, with minor modification, perfectly compatible with their ways of thinking and working; and that combining their ideas and techniques with his can create synergy and help them do even better the things they already do so well.

Most students or followers of Milton Erickson's teachings about psychotherapy come from the mental health community—psychiatrists, psychologists, and therapists from other mental health disciplines. For many of these professionals, the thought of working with alcoholics and addicts is akin to being sentenced to Siberia. Many professionals view such patients as untreatable or undesirable, or they have been "burned" by them, since addicted patients so often seem resistant and difficult, fail to keep appointments, and tend to be unreliable about paying for therapy.

I originally was a fairly representative member of the mental health community, but chance led me in a different direction: I *crossed over* into the alcoholism and drug addiction treatment community. In doing so, I learned that many of the things I was doing as a mental health person kept me from being effective with alcoholics and addicts. I also learned that attitudes I had clung to as a mental health person prevented me from seeing the many opportunities for excitement and satisfaction available in the addiction treatment field. As I struggled simultaneously to deal with addiction and to comprehend Erickson's ideas—which I pursued with the conviction that they must have a lot to offer to addictions treatment, but I wasn't yet sure what—I was eventually rewarded with what felt like an explosion of learning.

I hope to "turn on" members of the mental health community to a similar explosion of learning by showing them how Erickson's ideas can help them make sense of the addiction field. In particular, I hope to translate the concepts of Alcoholics Anonymous, which have often triggered a reflex rejection response in mental health professionals, by presenting them within the context of Erickson's (and other theorists') theories and therapeutic practices.

A NOTE ABOUT TERMINOLOGY

Three terms used in this volume need a few words of explanation, since they contain implications that might be missed otherwise, and the implications are central to the book. The terms are "chemical dependency," "Erickson-inspired," and "codependency."

CHEMICAL DEPENDENCY

This phrase cannot be found in the Diagnostic and Statistical Manual of the American Psychiatric Association (American Psychiatric Association, 1987), and professional journals and books make reference to the term rarely, if at all. Nevertheless, the term has a great deal of meaning since it is the identifying label of a burgeoning field, the treatment of alcoholism and drug addiction.

Until the last several years, treatment of alcoholism and drug addiction were widely disparate enterprises that went under separate headings and employed strikingly different approaches. I began in the field at that time, working originally in alcoholism (only) treatment. Gradually, as alcoholism programs discovered that alcoholics were often addicted to multiple substances and drug programs noticed that their clients often had drinking problems, the two fields began to merge. Now, where one used to find either alcoholism or drug addiction programs, there are Chemical Dependency programs. In deference to this reality, I will use this term throughout the book, even though it is not an "official" term.

ERICKSON-INSPIRED VS. ERICKSONIAN

During the past decade, a large number of "Ericksonian" therapists have produced numerous articles, books, and workshops on

"Ericksonian" approaches to hypnosis and therapy. Much of this work is valuable, but some of it seems to represent attempts to advance a therapist's personal interests by appearing to be connected or identified with Erickson, or to be more closely connected than one actually was. The fact that Erickson has become something of a cult figure makes this phenomenon even more tempting to potential pretenders.

While he lived, Erickson touched the lives of many—especially during his later years, when he conducted teaching seminars in his home. Since his death, the number of "students" of Erickson now seems to be increasing faster than it did during his life. Many of these "students" merely attended one or two seminars in Erickson's home. Even those who learned a great deal from Erickson during his later years nevertheless knew him only during those later years, and not at a time of his life when he was at his most active, creative, and dynamic.

Erickson often admonished students at his seminars not to imitate him (Personal Communication). Instead, he told them to incorporate what he had to show them about therapy and use it to improve their own individual styles. To imitate him, he felt, would deprive them of the opportunity to use their inner resources and expand their unique potentials. In other words, according to Erickson, to attempt to be an "Ericksonian therapist" would be to violate one of his most basic tenets about psychotherapy.

I have chosen not to be an imitator of Erickson, and my own personal connection with him consisted of attending two week-long seminars at his house in Phoenix, as well as interviewing him alone for a day in his home. Therefore, I feel uncomfortable applying the term "Ericksonian" to myself. Instead, I prefer to use the term "Erickson-inspired." This term clearly delineates my relationship to Erickson and his ideas. Most of the therapeutic approaches I describe here are not Erickson's, even though some of them "feel" somewhat similar to his approaches. However, they were developed in creative spurts brought on and enhanced by exposure to him and his writings.

CODEPENDENCY

This term has recently come very much into vogue. I have seen or heard it used to refer to spouses of chemically dependent persons, children of chemically dependent persons, people who have been abused as children, people who have strong needs to act as caretakers or rescuers of others, people who have poor "boundaries," anyone who has problems in relationships, and people with almost every kind of compulsion, neurosis, character disorder, or impulse-control disorder. In fact, it has come to mean pretty much everything, and therefore just about nothing.

In spite of this difficulty, the term still has some usefulness left in it, provided it is defined narrowly and clearly. Codependency is closely related to, and was preceded by, "co-alcoholism," which originally referred to the set of problems besetting spouses, children, relatives, and close associates of alcoholics. When alcoholism gave way to chemical dependency, codependency replaced co-alcoholism. This relatively narrow meaning is preferred here. Thus, in this book, the word codependency refers to the syndrome of psychological, emotional, physical, social, and other related problems that arise as the direct result of being in a close relationship with a chemically dependent person; a person who is in such a relationship is a codependent.

COMMENTS ON THE EXPERIENCE OF WORKING LIKE ERICKSON

I am assuming that many therapists have reacted (or will react) the way I did upon discovering Erickson: by marveling at the things he did; feeling confused and bewildered and thinking that I was missing something, but I didn't know what; wondering how he or anyone could possibly do the things he did; wishing *I* could do them; and concluding that I would probably never be able to pull it off.

Nevertheless, I felt a need to learn all I could from or about Erickson, so I read everything I could get my hands on, took all available courses on hypnosis, and eventually met and learned from Erickson himself. Looking back, I now realize that I might have been more patient, because the learning process took place over a period of years.

Gradually, and to my pleasant surprise, I began to feel more and more sure of myself with regard to Erickson's ideas and therapeutic approaches. They made sense to me intuitively and felt comfortable and familiar, no longer hovering just beyond my grasp. They had become part of me and they began to creep into my work in unexpected ways. In contrast to previous learning experiences, in which I consciously studied, practiced, and mastered skills, I began to catch myself doing things that felt "Erickson-like." I didn't *decide* to do these things. Instead, they *emerged* without warning and seemed to do themselves through me.

One of the most important discoveries I made at this time had to do with the issue of planfulness. Erickson appeared to be more adept at planning and executing complex and artful therapeutic strategies than any other therapist. I hoped to learn how to plan the way he did, so I listened closely to his answer when someone asked him about this at one of the teaching seminars at his home. I was amazed when he said: "I never plan." Here was a paradox of major proportions. It was obvious that he planned, yet he denied planning. Erickson was never one to help resolve paradoxes, so I didn't ask him to. I just put aside my perplexity and kept listening.

Later, when my work began to feel Erickson-like, I found myself planning without planning, and the paradox resolved itself. This development occurred at a time when I was leading multiple-family therapy groups in an inpatient alcoholism treatment program. The groups were large, often with as many as 50 participants, plus a co-therapist, a nurse, and one or more trainees. These groups were difficult to manage, not only because of their size, but also because there was a great deal of turnover among the participants, and we often did not know who would be attending until the night of the meeting.

The staff met before every meeting for a planning session, then again afterwards for a wrap-up. In the planning sessions, we shared information about the status of our patients, their family members, and their relationships. Then, we came up with a plan for how we would approach the situation. Thus equipped, we marched down the hall to the therapy room, took our seats, and *did something entirely different.* Each time, what we did seemed intuitively right and greatly superior to the plan we had carefully developed and then abandoned.

This pattern became routine: Before every session, we planned a strategy, and in every session, we abandoned the strategy and employed a new approach that always appeared more cleverly crafted than the strategy we had planned in advance. There was a running joke about our planning sessions. We told new trainees and staff members to "Be sure you attend our meeting before the meeting, where we plan what we aren't going to do."

The subjective experience of working this way was extremely interesting. During the planning sessions, my behavior changed in a number of ways; some I was aware of, and others I know about only because my colleagues told me about them. I either became immobile and stared fixedly at a spot on the floor as we discussed the patients or I paced restlessly, deep in concentration. While walking to the meeting room, I was calm, confident, often joking with colleagues. Then, upon entering the meeting room, I was transformed, displaying a serious, intense expression, with flashing eyes, a more resonant voice, and slow, dramatic physical gestures.

When I began a meeting, I was often surprised by what I heard coming out of my mouth. Since it generally seemed to work and felt good, I didn't stop it. I let it flow and enjoyed observing and participating simultaneously. My words and actions were very complex and I was frequently unaware of many of the nuances of my behavior, relying on the reports of my colleagues to find out what I had been doing. My actions often appeared disconnected and confusing, but by the end of a session it usually became apparent that they had been leading methodically toward a prefigured result. I understood clearly what Erickson meant when he said that he did not plan. More and more, my therapeutic style was marked by that same combination of planfulness and spontaneity that so intrigued me about Erickson's work.

From that point to the present, my clinical work has been deeply affected by Erickson's teachings. I have carried Erickson's influence to several different settings, where, each time, my primary interest has been the treatment of addictive behavior: alcoholism, drug addiction, compulsive overeating, and related compulsive disorders. I know that Erickson's teachings can enrich therapeutic work with any patient population, but I believe that treatment of addictions and compulsions can be enriched in a special way.

ORGANIZATION OF THE BOOK

In the second chapter, I describe the connection between Erickson-inspired therapeutic techniques and the experience of "surrender" and explain why Erickson-inspired therapeutic approaches show such promise for chemical dependency treatment. In addition, I provide some material on a subject that, as far as I know, has never before been discussed in print: Erickson's own definition of psychotherapy.

The rest of the book is devoted to describing Erickson-inspired approaches to treatment of chemical dependency and related problems. Chapter 3 discusses individual change, with the goal of defining the changes that need to occur within an addicted individual and describing some approaches that can be applied in individual therapy. Chapter 4 presents Erickson-inspired methods for influencing group dynamics, and Chapter 5 describes similar approaches to family process. Finally, Chapter 6 discusses an assortment of issues, including the value of the 12 Steps, application of Erickson-inspired approaches to other addictions and other treatment modalities, some ethical issues, and the relationship of dissociation to addiction.

Throughout the book, the intention is to challenge the reader, stimulate creative thinking, and raise possibilities and questions, rather than simply to provide answers, formulas, or recipes. This book cannot be, nor is it intended to be, *the* definitive statement on how to apply Erickson's ideas and techniques to chemical dependency. Instead, I hope that the book will be a jumping-off point for many people to develop new and diverse ways of thinking about and helping chemically dependent people and those who suffer from related problems.

2

Chemical Dependency and Erickson-Inspired Approaches: An Overview

While still a newcomer to alcoholism treatment, I found myself surrounded—and my cherished psychological ideas assaulted—by people whose entire background in the field came from Alcoholics Anonymous (A.A.). Although I struggled at first against what I perceived to be A.A.'s simplistic, pseudo-religious approach, I eventually accepted that I could learn something from this curious program (Lovern, 1981). Once I allowed my mind to open, I discovered that A.A. contained a number of sophisticated psychological insights, and I became captivated with one of them in particular: the concept of *surrender*. The surrender experience, I eventually realized, was the key phenomenon, the essential foundation upon which recovery from addictions must be built.

As a therapist, I concluded that helping people achieve the surrender experience would have to be my primary goal, so I began to search for methods that could help me accomplish it. I found that, although many theorists and therapists agreed that surrender was important, no one had anything to say about *how to make it happen*. Then I discovered Erickson! He displayed a vast and exhilarating array of the most creative methods I had ever seen, and practically all of them could be thought of as ways of bringing about the surrender experience.

The theme of this chapter, then, is the applicability of Erickson's therapeutic methods to chemical dependency, and their efficacy in producing or facilitating surrender. In expanding on this central idea, the chapter contains, first, some thoughts about what chemical dependency is—that is, what must be surrendered; then, the history of the concept of surrender, showing how Erickson rightfully deserves a place there; and, finally, some material gained from a personal interview with Erickson in which he discussed, among other things, his definition of psychotherapy.

THE CHALLENGE OF TREATING CHEMICAL DEPENDENCY

Before a clinician can even begin to understand and deal effectively with chemical dependency, he or she must accept this one basic axiom: Chemically dependent people are *very* sick. They are deceptively sick—much sicker than they appear to be or believe themselves to be. This statement is not made as a moral judgment or a put-down. It is simply a fact that must be recognized and borne in mind during every professional interaction with a chemically dependent person in order to avoid losing one's way down the labyrinthian corridors of misperception, misunderstanding, manipulation, and frustration that lie in wait for anyone who attempts to help an alcoholic or drug addict.

In what ways is a chemically dependent person sick? First, there is the denial/delusion system (Johnson, 1980), which is a nearly impenetrable fortress constructed of a combination of psychological defense mechanisms and the effects of alcohol and drugs—including altered perception, dissociation, and memory blackouts. This system allows a chemically dependent person to become more and more out of touch with reality, while somehow hanging onto the ability to convincingly appear competent, rational, and right. Then, there is the gradually worsening cognitive impairment (summarized by Ryan & Butters, 1986) that the chemically dependent person learns to compensate for and cover up as it develops, which causes impaired judgment (which the chemically dependent person is unaware of due to the inability of impaired judgment to judge itself as impaired); faulty problem identification, goal selection, and overall planning; and a carefully contrived and maintained veneer of being "with it" that actually contains serious holes and gaps.

Chemically dependent people also typically lack the ability to deal adaptively with emotions (also described by Johnson, 1980), due to years of using chemicals, at first to avoid feeling negative affects, but eventually to avoid feeling any emotions at all. Chemically dependent people are also often immature, demanding, and dependent, and prone to acting on impulse because of the disinhibiting effects of the chemicals they use excessively. Impulsiveness leads to behavior that conflicts with one's conscience, resulting in serious moral problems. As all these problems worsen, they effectively short-circuit the normal processes of awareness and learning that would, if fully functional, tell the chemically dependent person that there is a problem that seriously needs attention.

In short, chemically dependent people tend to be out of touch with large portions of reality—hence the title of this book. To help them, therapy must break through a conviction that manages to survive even in the face of a powerful and uncompromising reality that contradicts it—that there is nothing wrong with *them*, but that other "people, places, and things" are the cause of their troubles.

COMPLIANCE

A major stumbling block to therapy is chemically dependent people's ability to *appear* to have relinquished their defenses and accepted their addictions, while they actually continue to inwardly believe themselves innocent of "all charges" relating to addiction. This ability, called *compliance* (Tiebout, 1953), often fools everyone, including themselves, and relieves them of the pressure they find themselves under in treatment to perform the awesome tasks of stopping all alcohol and drug use forever and changing their entire way of life. Some patients who are very good at compliance manage to graduate from treatment dripping with optimism and enthusiasm, having impressed everyone concerned and received sincere congratulations all around, but then go out and get loaded again, much to the surprise of their families, friends, and helpers—and even themselves.

DR. HARRY TIEBOUT AND ALCOHOLICS ANONYMOUS

Dr. Harry Tiebout was a psychiatrist with close ties to early members of Alcoholics Anonymous. He ran a hospital where many early A.A. members first attained sobriety, and he was the psychotherapist who treated Bill W., the cofounder of A.A., for his depression that emerged after several years of sobriety. Tiebout observed the phenomenon of compliance and wrote several articles about it (Tiebout, 1947, 1949, 1953), aiming to clarify the difference between compliance and true, at depth, cooperation with treatment, or "surrender."

Tiebout conceptualized compliance as the visible and conscious side of a conflict within the minds of alcoholics, in which an unconscious attitude persists that is drastically different from their conscious disposition. Alcoholics caught up in this conflict cooperate fully with treatment—and with other aspects of reality—on a conscious level, but stubbornly retain a quality of defiant resistance outside of their conscious awareness. The result of this conflict is the familiar pattern in which alcoholics appear to be recovering, while, in reality, they are simply waiting for an opportunity to return to active alcoholism.

Tiebout (1954) wrote about another unconscious phenomenon

certain to occur and very difficult to unseat. He called this phenomenon the "Ego"—intentionally written with a capital "E" to distinguish it from Freud's very different concept of "ego." Tiebout's "big E Ego" is more closely allied to the popular meaning of ego, implying grandiosity and self-centeredness. Tiebout defines Ego as a set of "immature traits" that begin in infancy and are carried into adulthood, including a feeling of being omnipotent and deserving of special privilege; great difficulty tolerating frustration; and very high drive, which causes one to jump into activity suddenly and impulsively.

The Ego is a carryover from the infant's feeling of power and importance, as exhibited by the urgent need to be fed and otherwise satisfied, that Freud described with the phrase: "his majesty the baby." According to Tiebout, alcoholics somehow retain a large measure of this attitude of kingly—or queenly—sense of entitlement and impatience in their unconscious minds, where it stays alive or, after seeming defeat, reemerges resiliently regardless of consequences. Instead of maturing out of this attitude as a result of repeated exposure to reality, alcoholics often learn to project a veneer of agreeableness and charm that gives lie to their actual power-driven, regal feelings. This veneer helps them to cope with reality on at least a superficial level, while shielding the unconscious, infantile attitude from change. Compliance is obviously a part of this veneer.

EARLY A.A. AND SURRENDER

The issue of surrender is at the very core of the philosophy of Alcoholics Anonymous. Several currents of psychological thought converged in A.A. to form this belief. Some of the thinkers include Dr. Tiebout, William James (1958), and Carl Jung (1968). The history of A.A. begins with Jung's encounter with one of his patients, Roland H. (Alcoholics Anonymous, 1957; W., 1979):

Roland, a successful American businessman, traveled to Switzerland in the early 1930s for treatment of his alcoholism by

Dr. Jung. Approximately a year later, he completed the therapy with high hopes, yet he was drunk again within a short time. Roland returned to Switzerland to ask what had gone wrong, and Jung's response shocked him: He said he believed that alcoholics of Roland's type were *utterly hopeless*, and that his only chance of recovery lay in what he called a "vital spiritual experience." By this he meant a comprehensive "rearrangement" within a person of all ideas, emotions, attitudes, and basic motives (Alcoholics Anonymous, 1957). He suggested that Roland return to the United States and involve himself in a religious group of his choice, in hopes that doing so might bring about such an experience.

Actually, Jung often encouraged his patients to join religious groups. In a 1935 lecture (Jung, 1968), he stated that several of his patients had gone to the Oxford Group movement (an arm of which eventually became A.A.) "with my blessing!" He regarded religions as "psychotherapeutic systems" which had the goal of helping people detach from external objects, such as people, ideas, or situations, so that their "center of gravity" is in themselves instead of being invested in some object (or, by extension, some drug or drug-induced experience) on which they depend.

Roland followed Dr. Jung's instructions carefully. He became involved in the Oxford Group movement, which was a nondenominational organization active at that time in the United States that aimed to revive the spirit of early Christianity by practicing self-examination, admission of character defects in group meetings, making restitution for past wrongs, and basing one's direction and decisions on spiritual guidance received through prayer. And then it happened! Roland experienced the kind of internal reorganization that Jung had described, and he became unshakably sober. Soon, he began sharing this experience with other alcoholics, including one named Ebby T., who also became sober by having a vital spiritual experience. Ebby eventually visited one of his old drinking buddies, a New York stockbroker named Bill W. (Thomsen, 1975).

Bill was skeptical at first about Ebby's notion of surrendering his will to God or a Higher Power, yet he was unable to stop thinking about it. Ebby's ideas simmered in the back of Bill's mind through several more days of continued drinking and finally came to fruition during Bill's last detoxification treatment at a New York hospital where Bill had been a regular customer. While reluctantly agreeing to admit Bill to the hospital, the trusted and respected Dr. William Silkworth pronounced Bill's condition *hopeless*, a verdict that threw Bill into a state of turmoil. Sitting on the edge of his bed, he remembered Ebby's suggestions and desperately sought guidance from "whatever God there *might* be."

The response was instantaneous and dramatic. As his desperation grew, he found himself crying out: "If there is a God, let Him show Himself! I am ready to do anything, anything!" (Alcoholics Anonymous, 1957) Suddenly, he found the room lighting up with a white light and felt an ecstasy that he could find no words to describe. He felt as if he were on a mountain top with a "wind of spirit" blowing through him, and it occurred to him that he was free. When this state of ecstasy finally subsided, he came out of it with a feeling of certainty that he would never again need to drink. He felt that he was in "another world, a new world of consciousness."

Following the experience, Bill remained sober and went on to become one of the cofounders of Alcoholics Anonymous. The other cofounder was Bob S., an Akron, Ohio surgeon, another Oxford Group member who became sober shortly after Bill visited him. A.A. is generally acknowledged to have been born when these two men met.

A vital spiritual—or conversion—experience was of central importance to Bill's and Bob's recoveries, and to the recoveries of countless subsequent A.A. members. The importance of the phenomenon led to its incorporation in the first three of A.A.'s Twelve Steps of recovery (Alcoholics Anonymous, 1976):

STEP ONE: "We admitted we were powerless over alcohol—
   that our lives had become unmanageable."

STEP TWO: "Came to believe that a Power greater than ourselves could restore us to sanity."
STEP THREE: "Made a decision to turn our will and our lives
over to the care of God *as we understood Him.*

WILLIAM JAMES AND CONVERSION

Shortly after Bill's ecstatic experience in Dr. Silkworth's hospital,
Ebby gave him a copy of William James's, *The Varieties of Religious
Experience* (1958), a book based on James's 1901 lectures on the
psychology of religion. Bill found the book to be filled with
descriptions of experiences that were remarkably similar to his
own. Of particular interest were the sections dealing with the phenomena of *conversion.*

James defined conversion as an experience in which "the habitual center of [an individual's] personal energy," which existed in
deep, unconscious layers of the mind, is shifted and rearranged.
These rearrangements of mental systems often seem to occur suddenly or spontaneously. However, James saw them as actually following a period of "*ripening*" or unconscious undermining of the
habitual system. Once the mental system is prepared, a sudden
new experience or shock can unleash the rearrangement that had
been brewing all along, producing a drastically new mental structure, with very different ideas at its center. In short, James viewed
conversion as "subconsciously maturing processes eventuating in
results of which we suddenly grow conscious."

James saw conversion as a naturally occurring, adaptive process,
in which an individual strives for change at two levels, conscious
and unconscious. The goals and efforts operating at the two levels
differ and may come into conflict. While unconscious changes are
ripening and moving toward a prefigured result, the person may
interfere with the process by conscious efforts.

In other words, James believed that a person could block the
unconscious healing process by trying to impose conscious, willful
control over it. To do so, according to James, would be to rely upon

a *less effective* means of solving one's problems. James felt that when unconscious processes are at work on a problem the "better self" is in charge. He saw conscious approaches as being clumsy and capable only of vaguely aiming at the solution from the outside, whereas the unconscious self is capable of actually being the "organizing center." For this unconscious better self to operate unimpeded, it is necessary for the "conscious self" to relax, yield, or *surrender.*

Bill and other early A.A. members took James's perspective on self-surrender and conversion seriously and made it a cornerstone of A.A.'s philosophy of recovery. The contribution of other influences and theories were overlaid on this basic foundation.

GREGORY BATESON AND SCHISMOGENESIS

Gregory Bateson (1971) wrote a very interesting analysis of Alcoholics Anonymous, which focused on the concept of the alcoholic's *epistemology*—the "body of habitual assumptions or premises implicit in the relationship between man and environment." According to Bateson, a person's epistemology exists at "levels of the mind [which are] prelinguistic and . . . coded in *primary process,*" that is, unconscious. Something in the alcoholic's epistemology is "wrong" and needs to be corrected: He or she is caught up in a symmetrical "schismogenesis," an escalating conflict between self and "other" in which the alcoholic struggles to conquer and control, first alcohol, then authority, other people, and eventually reality itself.

The solution is "a dramatic shift from this symmetrical habit" to a complementary view of the alcoholic's relationship to others and to all of reality. Simply stated, the alcoholic must stop being *pitted against* reality and become *a part of it.* How this shift occurs "is complexly related to the experience of the double bind." Bateson cites Dr. Silkworth's (the doctor who pronounced Bill W. hopeless) description of alcoholism—*"the obsession of the mind* that compels us to drink and *the allergy of the body* that condemns us to go mad or die"—as a double bind which forces the alcoholic "back and back to the point at which only an involuntary change in deep unconscious epistemology—a spiritual experience—will make the lethal description irrelevant."

HOW ERICKSON'S WORK FITS IN WITH CONVERSION AND SURRENDER

For students of Erickson, much of the foregoing material on conversion and surrender will have seemed quite familiar, and for good reason. Bypassing conscious limitations to facilitate change at an unconscious level is the essence of Erickson's approach to psychotherapy. As Erickson (1977) stated:

> The patient doesn't consciously know what the problems are, no matter how good a story he tells you, because that's a conscious story. What are the unconscious factors? You want to deal with the unconscious mind, bring about therapy at that level, and then translate it to the conscious mind. (p. 21)

How *does* one bring about therapy at the unconscious level of a chemically dependent person's mind? Therapists who worked prior to Erickson, or who were unaware of his methods, had little to offer on this subject. Some occasionally stumbled upon therapeutic approaches which seemed to facilitate conversion or surrender experiences, such as the double bind, Jung's and Silkworth's statements (to Roland and Bill respectively) that alcoholism is a hopeless condition, and Johnson's (1980) interventions or planned interactions in which persons significant in a chemically dependent person's life present evidence to that person of the fact of his or her addiction in a way that overwhelms denial and ushers the person into treatment. In addition, Jung must have developed some techniques aimed at inducing spiritual experiences in patients, and perhaps specifically in alcoholics, but he never clearly spelled out any such techniques. Neither did Tiebout, though he must have thought hard about the subject and attempted many times to guide his patients toward surrender.

Then, into this vacuum stepped Erickson, who had a remarkable knack for developing creative methods that could overcome, bypass, or even take advantage of conscious distraction and resistance, while maximizing unconscious learning. In fact, another way of describing Erickson's work would be to say that one of his primary goals in psychotherapy was to produce conversion or surrender experiences.

When one considers the need of workers in chemical dependency treatment for ways to help people achieve surrender experiences along with the essence of Erickson's methods for achieving unconscious change, one cannot help but be impressed by the "fit" between these two previously uncombined activities. Yet we are only at the frontier of creating such a combination. Few attempts have been made so far, and these are still in their infancy. Chemical dependency treatment promises to gain greatly if more workers in the field seek inspiration from Erickson.

ERICKSON'S DEFINITION OF THERAPY

Many observers have been dazzled by Erickson's therapeutic virtuosity, but few have been able to describe or explain it in clear and simple terms. Erickson seemed not to want his work or ideas distilled into rules or recipes, and tended not to directly answer questions that could have led to such a reduction. As a consequence, Erickson's methods and strategies seem to many to be mysterious and cryptic. Therefore, any definitive statements he might have made about therapy are most welcome.

THE STORY OF JOE

To understand Erickson's unique definition of therapy, it will help to first go over one of his teaching stories, the story of Joe the convict (briefly summarized from a personal communication, 1978):

> Joe was a criminal who had terrorized the small, Wisconsin farming community where Erickson lived as a boy. Joe was no ordinary criminal, as Erickson learned later when he read Joe's records while working for a time in the prison in which Joe had been incarcerated. The list of crimes for which Joe had been convicted was very long, and in prison Joe had been completely incorrigible, as evidenced by the fact that he spent more time in solitary confinement than any prisoner ever had.
>
> When Joe was released from prison, he headed back to town and immediately resumed his criminal career. Several storekeepers noticed large items missing as early as the morning after his return. Fear of Joe spread rapidly.
>
> That Saturday, there was to be a dance, which in that small town was the major social event. Joe decided that he wanted to go to the dance, and he brashly invited the town's most sought-after young woman, Edie, the attractive daughter of a wealthy rancher who lived on the outskirts of town. When Joe swaggered up to her, blocked her path, and asked if he could take her to the dance, Edie smiled and said: *"You can if you're a gentleman."*
>
> The next morning, all the items that had been reported stolen reappeared, and there were no more thefts. When Saturday arrived, Joe appeared at Edie's house and escorted her to the dance in a most gentlemanly manner. He was clean, neat, and polite, and he and Edie danced almost every dance.
>
> Soon after the dance, Joe approached Edie's father and asked for a job. Edie's father hired Joe and allowed him to sleep in the barn. Joe worked hard every day from sunrise to hours past sunset, and when his work was done on the ranch, he often helped other ranchers and farmers with their heavy jobs. He studied and improved his reading and writ-

ing, and he began to attend church. Eventually, he earned the right to sleep in the house instead of in the barn. Finally, after several years of honest work, he married Edie.

Joe became a strong advocate of education, and he eventually became the town's Superintendent of Schools. Over the years, he managed to change the town's attitude toward education, from believing that high school and college educations were useless to seeing most of the town's young people complete high school and many go on to college—including Erickson. He helped the town and its people in many other ways, including inviting ex-convicts, as part of their rehabilitation, to live and work on his ranch.

The essence of this story is that Joe made a remarkably dramatic change in his life. He was transformed from an incorrigible convict to a hardworking, upstanding, model citizen.

What accounted for Joe's dramatic change? Erickson attributed it to *psychotherapy*. Erickson did not mean by this that Joe kept appointments in an office with a mental health professional. He meant that Joe had a crucial experience, a simple event that by chance challenged Joe to change. It happened when Edie told him: "You can if you're a gentleman."

AN INTERVIEW

The following is a partial transcript of an interview with Erickson, which contains a discussion about psychotherapy using the story of Joe as a focal point:

> *JDL:* Dr. Erickson, I'd like to discuss your ideas on psychotherapy. The story of Joe shows that you have a very different understanding of therapy than most of us have been taught. First of all, what is your definition of psychotherapy?

MHE: To help the patient achieve a fairly clear understanding of a simple goal in life that suits the person as a unique individual.

For example, Joe was a big man on the farm. He could pitch a big forkful of hay or grain. He had plenty of opportunities to contend with weight, use his strength, and get that tired feeling that says I've done a good day's work.

JDL: That was his goal.

MHE: I assumed it was, the way he responded to Edie. She was obviously a simple country girl. And Joe looked and had seen plenty of different kinds of people in the prison: the city hoodlum, the country rube, weaklings. The farm offered him plenty of challenges every day. And Edie gave him a challenge. And a very powerful challenge. Joe knew he was just a no-good convict. And Edie challenged him: "You can if you're a gentleman." She didn't know what she was saying. And that was the enormous talent. He just looked upon himself as a convict. You see, no matter how simple the wording is, it can be very, very complex in its meanings.

And of course his first response was: He showed her he could be a gentleman by returning stolen goods. That was returning them to others. He had to show her directly. And he took a job as hired man. He worked from sunup to long after sundown seven days a week. That's a real challenge. It was for fifteen dollars a month. And he slept in the barn with the cows and the horses.

People understand so much more than they know they understand. Edie's father knew what he wanted. He knew that Joe was an ex-convict. He challenged Joe. He made a concession: You want to be part of the family, you sleep in the barn. And he was offering Joe an opportunity to climb socially—a challenge, and was very forcible at putting Joe in his place, as a mere animal.

JDL: It was also a challenge to become the Superintendent
of Schools?

MHE: Mm-hmm. There were a lot of beautiful challenges
that Joe got. And by the belief that high school education was no good, Joe too got a challenge to show that
education was good. Joe encouraged high school and
college.

So much more could be said about Erickson and his approaches
to psychotherapy that attempting to do so in this book would
quickly cause it to lose track of its intended focus on chemical
dependency treatment. Therefore, the reader who is interested in
learning more about Erickson is referred to volumes by Haley
(1967, 1973, & 1985) and Erickson & Rossi (1979), among many
other fine works.

3

The Dynamics of Surrender: Approaches to Individual Change

THE EXPERIENCE OF ADDICTION AND RECOVERY

Inducing a chemically dependent person to surrender involves "shaking up" the relationship between conscious and unconscious processes. This relationship is a peculiar and paradoxical one that seems most readily explained by use of the metaphor of conscious and unconscious minds, as Erickson did. Even though the unconscious mind is the vastly more powerful and creative of the two, it tends to be willing to take direction from the conscious mind, which it also tries to humor and protect. Often, the unconscious mind has to work very hard to protect the conscious mind from having its feelings hurt, a feat it sometimes accomplishes by keeping certain facts and emotions outside of conscious awareness. At other times, it does this by acceding to the conscious mind's demands, even though doing so can cause problems that are much worse than hurt conscious feelings.

From this point of view, many people's problems may be seen as stemming from overreliance on conscious processing. Trying to control their problems consciously succeeds only in locking them into a rigid and self-perpetuating pattern. When that approach begins to fail, they respond by trying the same thing harder, instead of allowing their more flexible, creative unconscious mind to take command. As long as their conscious mind wants to stay in control, their unconscious mind allows it. Solutions that work are not possible until conscious control is relinquished, bypassed, or incapacitated.

Many of Erickson's approaches to both hypnosis and therapy consisted of methods designed to induce his patients to surrender conscious control, or, when they would not or could not surrender control, to circumvent, confound, or neutralize conscious control. He then formed an alliance with the unconscious mind, often taking into account its need to protect the conscious mind. Then, he and the unconscious mind worked cooperatively to arrive at solutions that would have been impossible to achieve with the conscious mind alone.

With chemically dependent patients, the overall goal is essentially the same. Conscious efforts to resolve alcohol and drug problems, which usually consist of applying willpower in an effort to control and enjoy the consumption of these substances rather than learning how to live without them, need to give way to creative, unconsciously developed solutions. A therapist can often deal with this situation successfully by talking past or around a chemically dependent patient's conscious mind, directly to the creative unconscious mind and cooperating with the creative forces there to break the stalemate and facilitate recovery. At the same time, the therapist should offer something of use and interest to the conscious mind, thus keeping it occupied and out of the way.

One way to communicate in this way is to take advantage of chemically dependent patients' need and desire for a conscious, intellectual understanding of their addiction and the changes that happen inside themselves as they recover. A therapist can offer explanations that satisfy the conscious intellect but also provide a structure for the unconscious mind, pointing out ways that would be productive for it to change. A number of such explanations exist, most of which are variations on a common theme. Variations of the standard message are made in order to tailor the explanations to the needs of the patient. Below is a script of some of the central ideas that are most helpful to get across to patients.

First, powerlessness is described in an effort to open patients' minds to the Twelve Steps, which begin with an admission of powerlessness:

> You may be having difficulty with the idea of powerlessness. Let me explain it to you. One of the most troublesome symptoms of chemical dependency is the belief that you don't have it. You won't want to go to the trouble to recover from something that you don't have—or that you don't believe that you have. And, even if you do believe that you have it, your belief may be only partial. Furthermore, even if you think you believe completely that you are addicted, you may not understand completely what it means to be addicted, and, therefore—since you don't know exactly what to believe—you can't completely believe it. Finally, you may be convinced that you believe that you are addicted, but you are aware only of your *conscious* belief. You may have a completely different belief in your unconscious mind. And you can be sure that your unconscious belief is the more powerful of the two.
>
> In order to recover, you must believe that you are addicted. So, how do you come to believe something? How does *anyone* come to believe something? Have you ever tried to convince someone of something? No matter how logically you demonstrate the facts to people, if they don't want to believe it, they won't. You can't argue someone into a belief; you can't force someone into a belief; you can't beg someone into a belief. Either he will, or he won't. In other words, you don't know how to make anyone—including yourself—believe anything.

And we're just talking about conscious belief. If you don't know how to change someone's, or your own, *conscious* beliefs, you'll find it much more difficult—if not impossible—to change *unconscious* beliefs. That's the problem: One reason you are powerless is that you don't know how to change your beliefs.

Another thing you are probably powerless over is the little voice in your head that tells you to drink or use. I'm sure you have experienced those seemingly innocent little thoughts, like: "Go ahead. One won't hurt." Or: "I've been good all day. Now I can have one as a reward." Or: "I've worked hard. I really deserve one." Or: "It's not a problem. I can quit any time." And chances are that, when you experienced these thoughts, they felt as if they were your own. But they weren't. They were put into your head by your addiction.

Every addict has had these thoughts or something just like them—and many more similar ones. That includes addicts and alcoholics, cigarette smokers, compulsive overeaters, and others. These thoughts, which always seem like our own and which we hear in our mind in our own thinking voice, have but one goal: to keep us having that "one more" drink, joint, pill, line, cigarette, or twinkie. I remember when I quit smoking. My little voice kept at me and kept at me, trying to get me to smoke. It used every trick of salesmanship in the book. Finally, after I had somehow managed to say "No" to it long enough for it to realize that I wasn't going to smoke, it said: "O.K., you win. Now you can eat." And, of course, I did.

When people persistently say "No" to the little voice, an interesting change takes place. The voice that used to sound just like our own thoughts begins to sound *un*like us. It becomes clearly foreign. It is unmasked, and we see—or hear—it for what it is: the voice of addiction. Only then do we begin to have an idea of what we are up against. Only then do we get a glimpse of the incredible subtlety, resourcefulness, and power of addiction—why they say in Alcoholics Anonymous that alcohol is "cunning, baffling, powerful."

Addiction is actually able to play its messages on our own inner "sound systems." It is as if it has tied and gagged the disk jockey at the local radio station and is doing a perfect impression of his or her voice. But that is only the beginning. Not only does it do a flawless impression of our thinking voice, but it tailors its messages to us in a way that is based on our deepest, innermost fears, angers, and hurts. It knows how we feel about things, and it knows where our "emotional buttons" are. It pushes these buttons, and then it takes advantage of our reactions to get us to practice our addictions. It knows its way around the inside of our head better than we do.

Addiction puts these thoughts into our head constantly, usually using subtle and reasonable, though faulty, logic to get us to do what it wants. It is only a matter of time before we act on one or more of these messages. If we believe or act on one message, we are more likely to act on subsequent messages. Gradually, the addiction assumes greater and greater control, both of our thinking and of our behavior. Our own thinking is eventually drowned out by addictive thinking, and our behavior is dominated by it. Drugs and alcohol make us even more susceptible to addiction's warped reasoning, and we fall completely under its control. It becomes more bold in its control of our activities. We become automatons run by our addictions. We cease to have a mind of our own.

If this description frightens you, it should. It sounds like something out of science fiction, such as *Invasion of the Body Snatchers*, or like the picture of demon possession shown in *The Exorcist*. Looking at addiction in this way shows how tricky addictions are, and how we are completely at their mercy. There is no way that we can defeat a force like this by unaided, conscious reason or willpower. In fact, our conscious intellect and willpower are likely to become tools that addiction uses to assume even greater control over our life. We are truly powerless over addiction. When you get that, you'll be ready to start on your recovery.

Next, they are given a description of the recovery experience. Again, the pointlessness of trying to consciously control or manage the process is emphasized:

You can't control your recovery from chemical dependency. You have to experience it. You will want to understand it intellectually, plan it, and make it speed up or slow down to a comfortable pace. But you won't be able to do that. It's a process, like grieving and pregnancy are processes. And all you can do is let the process run its course. You can interrupt it at any time, and make it stop; but then you'll just wind up back in the progression of the disease, feeling like you did before, only worse. That's an absolute guarantee: It will always get worse.

At any given point in time, you have only two choices: the disease or recovery. You know what the disease is like. As long as you are in the disease, it just keeps on advancing, destroying your body, your mind, your family, your job, your dignity, your self worth—all the while telling you that it's your best friend, that you should trust it. If you don't like the disease, your only other choice is recovery. But recovery is uncomfortable, uncertain. You never know what to expect. Your disease, as ugly and malignant as it is, offers certainty. You always know what to expect. That's one of the reasons that the majority of people who have the disease choose it over recovery. I'm hoping that you will have the courage to choose recovery.

I'd like to tell you about recovery, so that you will know what to expect. That way you will be less likely to give up on it when it starts to get uncomfortable. I call recovery "*going sane*." It feels just like going insane, only it goes in the opposite direction. It's like the difference between taking a plane from Los Angeles to New York, as opposed to taking a plane from New York to Los Angeles. Both trips feel exactly the same with your eyes closed, even though they are going in opposite directions.

The first thing that happens when you stop practicing your addiction is withdrawal. Your body goes through a period of intense physical craving. You get restless. If you're standing up, you want to sit down. If you're sitting down, you want to stand up. You hurt all over. Even your hair hurts. You have extreme mood swings and crazy emotions. One minute you're laughing, and the next minute you're crying. You can't think straight. You might even have more serious symptoms, like hallucinations or seizures, so you need good medical supervision. You're a complete physical, mental, and emotional wreck. This period lasts anywhere from a few days to a few weeks before it finally wears off.

After the withdrawal is over, you start to feel pretty good. This stage lasts until your feelings come back. Where are they coming back from? From where they have been buried. Drugs and alcohol make you feel better. When addiction sets in, a major change occurs. Instead of making you feel better, they make you feel *less worse*. They do that by making painful feelings go away. But they don't really go away. They go into hiding. They build up inside you and wait for an opportunity to be felt. The more they build up, the more you need to drink, use drugs, and engage in compulsive behaviors to keep them down.

After you stop drinking and using, all these buried feelings start to come up. They don't come up in any orderly fashion. They all come up at once. Just like white light is all the colors of the spectrum combined together, you feel "white emotion." You don't know if you're angry, scared, sad, or what—because you're all of them at once. It's kind of like when I quit smoking and my sense of smell returned. Everything and everybody stank! I could smell body odors in elevators and garbage in cans a mile away. It was almost more than I could stand. But after awhile I got used to it, and now I depend on my sense of smell. While it was gone, I didn't know what I was missing. Now it's an important tool for telling me about the world. Emotions are like that too.

Having emotions again is like switching from black and white TV to color.

Another big problem with emotions is the fact that you aren't used to having them. While you were practicing your addiction, alcohol and drugs took care of your feelings. The longer you drank and used, the more out of practice you became. Either you don't have the equipment for dealing with emotions, or it is so rusty that you don't know how to use it. When you get clean and sober, you get two whopping doses of feelings: all the feelings that you didn't feel while you were drinking and using, and all the normal emotional reactions that you have about the present. Wading through that mess is a difficult, time- and energy-consuming task.

At this point, a description is often added of the confusion that a patient is likely to encounter as part of recovery, emphasizing how positive and healthy that confusion is and encouraging the patient to accept it and let it happen. A script of this description is given later in this chapter.

Sometimes, patients are given the entire script (including the above and the part on confusion). More often, pieces of it are given when certain patients appear to need that particular information. For example, when a patient is experiencing an overwhelming outpouring of emotion, the description of the emotional part of the recovery experience often has a calming and reassuring effect and encourages the patient to "hang in there" and trudge through the experience, instead of terminating it by getting loaded.

MOTIVATION FOR TREATMENT

It is often said of alcoholics and addicts that they cannot begin to recover until they are "motivated" to do so. This prescription is very difficult—in fact, impossible—to meet, because one of the prominent symptoms of chemical dependency is the inability to know that one is addicted. How can someone who does not believe himself or herself to be addicted ever become motivated to recover?

A partial solution to this dilemma may consist of an alternate way to conceptualize motivation to recover. It is proposed that alcoholics' and addicts' *awareness of their pain* and their *willingness to do something to alleviate it* constitute adequate motivation for *treatment*. This motivation is not the same thing as motivation to *recover*. That is impossible, at least in the beginning. But this kind of motivation *is* possible and can be *used*. Using this motivation is an example of Erickson's technique of *utilization*, which will be discussed at greater length later in the chapter.

From the point of view outlined above, the object of the motivation has been changed, from "motivation to recover" to "motivation for treatment," because helping chemically dependent people is best done in stages. First, one needs to get the person into treatment, with or without motivation to recover. Then, once the person is in treatment, the larger task can begin of building in him or her the necessary motivation to recover.

Here, in line with this reasoning, is an operational definition of motivation for treatment: *Three drunk driving arrests, divorce papers, and an irate boss.* This is another way of saying that an alcoholic's or addict's motivation for treatment may be viewed as the culmination of a crisis. When addicts and alcoholics find themselves in uncomfortable or painful crises, they are likely to try to extricate themselves, to get demanding people off their backs, to placate those who have taken offense at their behavior, and to minimize threats to their freedom or their physical integrity.

Such unpleasant states of affairs can be utilized to good advantage to get chemically dependent people into treatment. All that is necessary is to convey to them that going into treatment is the only way to get out of the mess they are in. "Interventions" as described by Vernon Johnson (1980) and others are structured interactions that are designed to accomplish this exact result. An intervention counselor gathers together as many as possible of the people who can document the chemically dependent person's problems with chemicals, and who are in a position to place the chemically dependent person into an unpleasant situation, such as divorce, unemployment, or just plain guilt. Then, they offer treatment as the best way to avoid the dreaded consequences. At this point, the chemically dependent person finds his or her bags already packed, insurance coverage already verified, and a bed reserved at a treatment center. Interventions of this sort almost always work. That is, they almost always get the chemically dependent person into a treatment situation.

The formal, planned intervention should be viewed as a member of a broader, general class of opportunities for getting a chemically dependent person into treatment. It is the best orchestrated and surest method, but many other situations commonly arise that can be used effectively. A person cannot be chemically dependent for very long without getting caught in a wringer in some way or other. Typical examples are arrests for drunk driving, fighting, or domestic disturbances; poor job performance reports, excessive absences, or impending termination at work; separations, divorce, or reports of child abuse or neglect at home. When one of these crises occurs, an astute therapist or other helper can use it to channel the chemically dependent person into treatment. In fact, to fail to take advantage of this kind of crisis is a definite disservice, one that could have fatal consequences. When you are utilizing a crisis to get an addict into treatment, the process is much easier and more effective if the plan is backed by family members, employers, judges, or others who are in a position to influence the chemically dependent person. The situation should be set up so that the chemically dependent person can get out of the jam only by seeking, participating in, and completing treatment.

For example, one approach that was quite successful was with patients who were referred by their attorneys, with the understanding that completing the program devised for them might convince the judge handling their drunk driving (or other alcohol- or drug-related) case to give them a lighter sentence than they might ordinarily expect to receive. They complied with this arrangement much more completely than drunk drivers typically comply with treatment to which they are sentenced. The difference is that this arrangement contained the possibility of getting out of something. When they are sentenced to a program, everything is already settled, so that complying with the program (as opposed to simply tolerating it until it is over) holds no promise of changing anything. Therefore, they often just "do time" until the sentence is over, instead of using the experience to assist in recovery from their addictions.

Highlighting and Challenging Low Motivation

Once a patient is in treatment, the issue of his or her motivation to recover needs to be addressed. *Highlighting* a patient's low motivation consists of comparing the patient's behavior in and attitude toward treatment with examples of other people and situations so that, when laid alongside these examples, his or her motivation appears to be blatantly, even ludicrously poor. *Challenging* a patient's low motivation consists of predicting certain behaviors that are likely to occur in an unmotivated patient or accusing the patient of being unmotivated, in a way that dares or challenges the patient to prove the therapist wrong.

It is appropriate to highlight a patient's low motivation when he or she has failed to follow the therapist's instructions (for example, to attend a certain number of A.A. meetings, complete a written assignment, etc.), or when the patient is reacting to treatment as if it were punishment for a crime rather than treatment of a disease. The following hypothetical interaction is an example of highlighting low motivation in therapy:

Therapist: Did you go to three A.A. meetings this week, as you committed to do?

Patient: Well, I had to work late Tuesday, and my kids needed a ride to the mall Wednesday, and blah, blah, blah (excuses and rationalizations).

Therapist: It sounds to me as if either you don't believe that your addiction is a disease or you don't realize how serious a disease it is.

Patient: Sure, it's a disease. And I know it's important. It's just that I've neglected my job and my family so much while I was drinking and using, that I have to make it up to them now while I'm sober.

Therapist: I can understand your feeling bad about having been irresponsible during your drinking and using years. But it's much more important that you do what it takes to stay clean and sober now than risk your sobriety by trying to make it up to your boss and family too soon. You'll be no good to them drunk or loaded. I hear you say that you believe that your addiction is a disease, but I don't think that you really believe it. Because, if you really believed it, you would be acting differently.

Patient: What do you mean?

Therapist: You're acting like your disease is a little character flaw that you can straighten out with good intentions and willpower. You're not acting like you have a progressive, terminal disease that will kill you if you don't do everything in your power to recover.

What if I were a kidney doctor instead of a psychologist (or chemical dependency counselor, etc.)? And suppose I told you that you needed dialysis three times a week, or else you would die. I think you would be a lot more serious about going for dialysis than you are about going to A.A. meetings.

Patient: Well, of course I would, but that's not the same. Kidney disease is a physical illness.

Therapist: And your addiction isn't a physical illness?

Patient: Well, I guess it is.

Therapist: You know it is. And it's a psychological illness. And an emotional illness. And an interpersonal illness. It's the ultimate disease. And it kills more people than kidney disease ever did. But I guess you'd rather die of addiction than of kidney disease.

Patient: O.K.! I get the message. I'll go to more meetings.
Therapist: We'll see. I have my doubts.
Patient: I give you my word. I promise.
Therapist: Right. I always believe an addict's promises. As I say, we'll see.
Patient: That's right. You will (angrily)!

There was a little challenge at the end of the example above. The patient was challenged to prove the therapist wrong after the therapist insinuated that the patient was not believable or trustworthy. Challenges can range from that one, which is relatively mild and gentle, to dramatic, extremely memorable ones. Consider the following vignettes, which illustrate the effects of challenges on individuals (although they occurred in group sessions). An excellent time to challenge a patient is when the patient is new to treatment. The challenge can be used to forge a strong commitment to action on the part of the new patient, while also uniting the patient with the group against the "offending" therapist.

Lick My Boot

While the inpatient group was interviewing a new patient, they inquired about his commitment to recovery. At this point, the therapist loudly and arrogantly interrupted to ask: "Tell me, Mr. Blank, are you willing to go to any length to get sober?"

The patient, looking somewhat confused but trying to appear believable, stated: "Yes, I am."

"*Any length?* repeated the therapist. "Are you sure?"

"Yes, of course."

To which the therapist replied: "O.K., then lick my boot!" (holding the sole of his boot into the air, facing the patient).

"What?" asked the patient incredulously, as the rest of the group, who had been through this process before, conspired with the therapist by saying and doing nothing.

"You heard me," said the therapist. "Come over here and lick the sole of my boot. You said that you're willing to go to any length. I want to see if you really mean it, so I'm telling you what one of the lengths is that you'll have to go to get sober. I'm your doctor, and that's my prescription for you. Come on over here and do it."

"No. I won't do it."

"Well. Now we know two things about you. We know how much of what you say we can believe, and we know how much you really want to get sober. And it looks like 'not much' on both counts. I hope the group can do something to help this guy, because I don't think the prospects are too good."

It does not portend well for a patient's treatment when he refuses to follow the first direction his doctor gives him after he is admitted to the hospital for treatment of a deadly disease. But that is what Mr. Blank did. The therapist's maneuver forced him into appearing to be both uncommitted to recovery and a liar. He had to admit, in his own mind, that he had been a bit cavalier and insincere in his original statement about being willing to go to any length to get sober. And he learned that he will probably be challenged to perform on any future public commitments he makes. The abrasive manner in which the therapist challenged Mr. Blank was likely to enhance any desire he may already have had to prove the therapist wrong in the future. The way to do that is to live up to his commitments and behave in a way that proves his commitment to sobriety.

Captain Hook

The situation is the same as before, with the group interviewing a new patient. Again, the therapist interrupts. This time, he inquires: "Mr. Blank, I'm curious about just how committed you are to sobriety. Would you for example, give up your right arm to get sober?" The patient, appearing somewhat shocked, began to attempt an answer: "Well, I think . . . I mean, that is . . ."

The therapist interrupted again, saying: "Oh, by the way, Mr. Blank, I'd like to introduce you to someone. Captain, would you please salute the new man?" At that moment, a patient who had lost his right hand and forearm in an accident and was now fitted with a prosthetic hook, raised his hook in the air and made it click open and shut.

Mr. Blank, already nervous about being in the hospital and fearful about what ordeals he might endure there, stared in disbelief at the man with the hook, momentarily overcome by the thought: "Omigod! They might make me give up my right arm in this place!" Then, he regained his composure and realized that, no, he would probably not have to give up an arm. Nevertheless, the impression was left in his mind that recovery from addiction was going to demand a serious commitment on his part.

Please note that the patient with the hook in this example actually enjoyed and benefited from the interaction. He learned to stop being as sensitive about his disability, to see it with humor, and to discover that it made him special in a way, rather than just different. Other patients with visible disabilities or deformities might be harmed by the same sort of interaction, however, so care in such situations is strongly recommended.

UTILIZATION

Utilization is probably the most "Ericksonian" of Erickson's therapeutic approaches or techniques (Erickson, 1967a). He developed utilization techniques primarily to help patients achieve hypnosis who unconsciously wanted and needed to be hypnotized but who resisted so effectively at the conscious level that conventional hypnotic induction techniques were completely useless with them. Erickson overcame these patients' resistance by accepting and utilizing it instead of trying to take it on directly or tussling with it. Utilization is like a psychological form of judo, the Japanese martial art in which one overcomes a more powerful aggressor by using the aggressor's strength and force against him or her.

Utilization, in this context, consists of, first, discovering some trait, tenacious behavior, or strong attitudinal or behavioral tendency, that is often a problem or otherwise undesirable, and, second, instead of trying to fight it or get rid of it, *using* it as leverage to accomplish therapeutic change. Several traits exist in abundance among chemically dependent persons, any of which can be the basis of a utilization technique. Some of these traits are: rebelliousness and defiance; guilt; self-hate and low self-esteem; pain; need for excitement; and what Erickson called "convict honor." Examples below show how each of these traits can be utilized.

UTILIZING DEFIANCE

Before a therapist can utilize a patient's defiance, he or she should make sure that the patient is defiant *enough*. That is, the therapist needs to be able to count on the patient to make defiant responses from the beginning to the end of the therapeutic intervention. If a defiant response is not forthcoming at a crucial point, the intervention could backfire, leaving the patient even farther from ultimate cooperation with treatment than he or she was at the outset. To ensure defiance, the therapist can make him- or herself easier to defy. That is, the therapist can behave in an arrogant, impudent, rude, and demanding way, offering a tempting target for defiant resistance.

With some practice, a therapist can discover latent abilities (or employ traits or abilities that are not so latent, and might in other circumstances be thought of as problems in relating) that enable him or her to bring chemically dependent patients to heights of antagonism previously thought unattainable, and probably even feared by many therapists. Many therapists will find these behaviors difficult to perform at first, since they are completely contrary to the gentle, caring, and affirming manner that most therapists generally maintain. There is also the danger that "letting out" this kind of behavior could be too enjoyable, or meet too many unconscious needs of the therapist and thus create a therapeutic monster. Therefore, caution and prudence are strongly recommended; therapists are urged to maintain a balance by retaining the ability to be gentle, soft, and vulnerable, while also learning to be outrageous and antagonistic. The resulting wide, dynamic interpersonal range will eventually allow the therapist to be more helpful to more kinds of patients.

Some behaviors which are guaranteed to heighten defiance and antagonism include facial expressions such as glaring, sneering, pouting, rolling up one's eyes after a patient states an opinion, and curling one's lip while saying how incredibly sick the patient is; talking about one patient to another patient in the first patient's presence, as if the first patient were a child; inferring or implying gross insults without actually coming out and saying them or naming the target; and flaunting one's authority (for example, by dramatically and pompously smoking a long, fat cigar during a group session in which the patients are not allowed to smoke). Many therapists will be able to create (or recreate) antagonizing interactional styles by remembering and drawing on the verbal combat skills that most early adolescents are exposed to in peer interactions at school.

The examples below show some ways that defiance can be utilized. The first example demonstrates one way to arouse and enhance defiance, and then predict the symptom and make a bet with another patient that the first patient will do as predicted. The second example shows the power of predicting a relapse. Before we proceed to these examples, however, a note of caution is needed.

The therapeutic maneuver of increasing defiance should be used only with extreme care. Careless use can cause serious problems for both patient and therapist. If therapists exercise inadequate precautions, their patients may storm off and never return for help from them or from any professional. The final outcome for such patients could be disaster or death. Therapists face the risk that outsiders, supervisors, or overseers unfamiliar with the rationale for this technique may construe it as unethical behavior, resulting in their facing charges that they verbally abuse their patients.

What specific measures constitute adequate precautions vary with the characteristics of the patient and the therapeutic situation. As a general rule, heightening defiance and similar techniques should be employed only if there is little to lose anyway, and no other approach is likely to work; if experienced clinical intuition indicates that there is a good chance that it will help; if the object of derision is the patient's disease, and not the patient's person; and if the therapist's message of contempt is balanced in some way by respect and concern for the patient's dignity.

In the first example below, the patient was already obviously defiant, and he was at the point of walking out and giving up on recovery at the moment that the technique was employed. Therefore, there was little to lose in heightening his defiance. In addition, the therapist felt certain, based on clinical intuition and long experience with previous chemically dependent patients, that, if this patient's defiance were heightened, he could be influenced to rebel against the therapist, and thereby be influenced to stay in treatment. Finally, the interaction occurred in a group that had been guided for months to develop an atmosphere of strong, tangible support and caring for its members. The therapist could count on the group to offer loving concern to the new patient in sufficient measure to counter the therapist's rude and antagonizing behavior.

The Bet

A new patient, Phil, who had recently been detoxified, appeared for his first day of outpatient treatment. It was obvious that Phil did not want to be there. Also, additional inquiry indicated that his wife had threatened to divorce him unless he did something about his drinking problem. His strategy appeared to be to find something wrong with the program, so that he could justify dropping out and thereby meet both his wife's demand that he do something about his drinking and his own addictive desire to do nothing about it. His behavior confirmed this impression, as he was noted to be minimizing the severity of his own drinking-related problems while expressing strong negative opinions of the treatment program and its way of doing things.

Phil's critical attitude continued to build until it reached a crescendo, at which point he stated openly that he didn't think that this program was for him, that he would prefer to "quit on [his] own," and that he didn't need to sit around in group meetings "with a bunch of low life slobs." He began to stir in his chair as if he were ready to stand up and leave.

At this point, the therapist began a conversation with another patient about Phil, talking about Phil as if he were not in the room, much as parents sometimes discuss their children in their children's presence, and using his most aggravating, sarcastic tone of voice. "Well, Bob, I think this guy is one of the sickest I've ever seen. I usually don't feel hopeless about an alcoholic right after I meet him, but this guy is one *sick sucker* What do you think about that?"

Bob, whom the therapist selected because of his predictable response to questions of this type, replied: "I don't think he's hopeless. I talked the same way when I got here."

The therapist feigned an arrogant attitude and unleashed a flurry of statements that Phil could be expected to take as being about him (but not *to* him, or directly naming him) that were designed to raise his defiance level: "Yeah, you're right; you did say some of the same things this guy is saying, but I don't think you were such a big, whining baby. You, at least, were able to stand up for yourself. This one doesn't seem to be a man at all. He's just tied to mama's apron strings. I expect him to start blubbering any minute."

Phil, feeling attacked, now tried to protest or fight, saying "What did you call me?"

The therapist replied, still refraining from addressing Phil directly, instead theatrically addressing the entire group: "Did anybody hear me using any names? I didn't call anybody anything. I was just speaking in general terms. If anybody wants to take it personally, that's his problem. Now, the group seems to have a guy who doesn't know when to shut up. Doesn't he realize that children should only speak when they're spoken to?" When Phil tried several additional times to interrupt the conversation between the therapist and Bob, the therapist repeated, in a sarcastic manner: "The group seems to have a problem with a guy who doesn't know how to hold his tongue. Now, as I was saying before I was so rudely interrupted . . ."

Bob continued to take exception to the therapist's characterization of Phil: "Give the guy a break, Doc. I don't think he's any sicker than I was. He's got a chance. I think we can help him, and I think he's got a good chance to make it."

The therapist continued with his doubts: "He's got a chance to make it all right. He'll make it to the liquor store or the gin mill on the corner. I seriously doubt that we will be able to help him. He doesn't want our help. The first thing he's going to do when he gets out of here today is go get loaded. And then he'll be too cowardly to show up back here again—which would suit me fine, because I can't think of a more disgusting sight than that face showing up here day after day."

"But," Bob protested, "you yourself said that you don't give up on an alcoholic 'until he's being patted in the face with a shovel.' I say that Phil *will* show up, and he *will* get better."

"All right," said the therapist. I'll tell you what I'll do. You're obviously convinced that he's going to show up here tomorrow, so I see a way to get a free cup of coffee out of you. I only bet on a sure thing, and I love a sucker. So I'll bet you a cup of coffee that he won't be back tomorrow."

"You're on," said Bob.

"Remember," said the therapist, "I like my coffee black. I

won't even bother to get myself a cup of coffee tomorrow morning, because I know that you're going to lose this bet. Don't even check to see if he's here. He won't be. Just put my name on it, and deliver it to the desk out front."

"Hah!" said Bob. "I'm going to win this bet, and when I do, I'll share my cup of coffee with Phil. We'll both enjoy making a fool out of you."

The next morning, the patient whom the therapist bet would fail to return arrived triumphantly at the therapy session, where he was greeted by the patient with whom the therapist made the bet. Together, they demanded payment from the therapist, who settled the bet while displaying mock disbelief and amazement. The patient continued to attend without further inducements, except for the therapist to occasionally remark offhandedly, with a slight tone of (mock) begrudging admiration, that he or she was "sure surprised" that a given patient was still attending. If, on the other hand, the patient seemed likely to drop out of treatment after one bet, and was still inclined to be defiant, the therapist could make another bet and continue to do so as long as necessary, until the patient was locked into treatment by other forces, such as the acceptance and camaraderie of his peers.

In the second example, the therapist did nothing to heighten defiance, since the patient was near completion of the program and had developed a more varied relationship with the therapist. If there was defiance, the therapist hoped, it was latent and unconscious, and it would arise later, along with the patient's urge to drink, when conditions favored the relapse that the therapist predicted.

The Predicted Relapse

Mike came to the hospital for alcoholism treatment from a small, remote town outside of the state. Prior to his discharge, he told of his plan to return home by bus, which was the only form of transportation available. Although Mike had

complied well with every formal aspect of treatment, the therapist had a nagging hunch that Mike still wanted, and was
likely, to drink. Therefore, during the last group meeting
before Mike's discharge, when the staff and group were going
over Mike's plans, the therapist made the following prediction:

"O.K., Mike. Your discharge plan sounds very good. But,
here's what I think you're *really* going to do. You're going to
get on that bus and ride out of town. And when the bus
makes its first stop, you're going to get out and buy a jug and
take a long pull on it and think to yourself, F__ k that hospital
and that group and that staff!' But, if I'm wrong, and you
don't drink at the *first* stop, then I'm sure that you'll get out
at the *second* stop, and buy a jug, and take a drink, and think
to yourself, 'F__ k that hospital and that group and that staff!'

"Now, I still might be wrong, and I don't know how many
times the bus stops. But I'm *absolutely certain* that, if you don't
do it at the first or the second stop, you're going to get out
at *one* of those stops and buy a jug and take a long drink and
think to yourself, 'F__ k that hospital, that group, and that
staff!'"

Approximately a year later, Mike was visiting in town, and he
came to the hospital to let us know with great pride that he was
still sober. He enjoyed telling us the story of his ride home:

I got on the bus feeling great and looking forward to getting
home. We drove for hours and then the bus finally stopped
for a rest break. Without thinking, I got up out of my seat
and headed for the door, planning to buy a bottle. Then it
hit me what Dr. Blank had said just before I left, and I
thought, "That damn Dr. Blank said I would do this. I'll be
damned if I'll prove him right!" So, I rode on to the next
stop. Again, I started to go out and get a drink, but the same
thought stopped me. That went on all the way home, during
every stop, until I found myself arriving home sober, with my

wife and kids waiting for me at the bus station. I hated that Dr. Blank, but now I think I wouldn't be sober if it hadn't been for him.

UTILIZING GUILT

One of the paradoxes of chemical dependency is the fact that many addicts and alcoholics behave as if they had no guilt, thereby causing many of them to be mislabeled as sociopaths, while they are actually often wracked with such high levels of guilt that they suffer constantly from it. One of the emotional functions of drinking and using is to escape or avoid the feeling of guilt. However, this strategy backfires, because alcoholics and addicts tend to do things while under the influence that they subsequently feel even more guilty about. As the addictive cycle continues, guilt becomes a sensitive issue, much as a thumb becomes sensitive when one accidentally hits it over and over with a hammer. Once guilt has become a sensitive issue for a chemically dependent person, he or she will go to great lengths to avoid it. Therein lies the opportunity for utilization: to use the possibility or the threat of guilt as a motivator.

Guilt as a motivator is most useful in two situations. First, it is often the deciding factor in interventions, and second, it can be very useful in the group technique of "sacrifices" (Cutter, 1975).

Interventions were mentioned earlier in this chapter, so it is noted only briefly here that their effectiveness often hinges on effective utilization of guilt. One of the most effective methods is to make certain that children, if there are any, should speak last. That is because the children, describing with wide eyed innocence and undefended pain how they have been hurt, let down, and abandoned by their chemically dependent parent, are more likely than anyone else to arouse strong feelings of guilt in that parent. The point of greatest guilt is the time that the intervention counselor is most likely to elicit an agreement to enter treatment. This strategy often works, because the chemically dependent person is likely to do almost anything to escape or reduce the guilt.

A *sacrifice* is a decision by a group of chemically dependent patients to give up something in order to show their love and concern for a single patient. It is a constructive alternative to punishment when a single group member has violated a rule or behaved in a countertherapeutic manner. For example, if an individual who is responsible for cleaning the coffee maker fails to do so, the entire group might sacrifice coffee for 24 hours.

The decision to sacrifice must be made voluntarily. A sacrifice is a willing, loving giving up of something by a group of peers. If the staff were to require a sacrifice, it would not be a sacrifice as defined here. It would be punishment by authority, in this case punishment of the entire group instead of an individual. This approach would mobilize group pressure and focus it on the individual, but, because it is punishment imposed by authority, its primary effect would be to arouse hostility. A sacrifice, done correctly, arouses guilt. The patient who violates group rules, who might in the "real world" expect to be singled out and punished if caught (or worse, "chewed out" or "called on the carpet," and then given "one more chance"), instead faces a group of peers who willingly suffer for him or her. The patient's behavior thus causes an entire group to suffer, and the guilt is multiplied by the number of people who are affected. The whole tone of discipline is changed by the use of this technique. Whereas resistant, manipulative patients might otherwise try to get away with everything they can due to resentment of authority, they tend under this system to become very cooperative and responsible, and therefore more open to the possibility of recovery. A more extensive discussion of sacrifices may be found in the next chapter, which covers group processes.

UTILIZING LOW SELF-ESTEEM AND SELF-HATE

A chemically dependent person who is new in treatment may be expected to have terribly low self-esteem, but to keep this feeling from becoming outwardly visible. Instead, patients often present a facade of arrogance and grandiosity, coupled with strict perfectionism, reflecting their efforts to defend against and keep unconscious the deeply painful experience of self-hate and low self-evaluation. Occasionally, one sees newly recovering chemically dependent people behaving as if they loathe themselves, but one cannot be sure whether their expression of this feeling is genuine, or if it is calculated to arouse pity and compassion in the person with whom they are interacting, as a way of "softening up" that person for manipulation.

One cannot "give" self-esteem to an alcoholic or addict. Although unconditional positive regard may have salutary effects on other patient groups, it is much more difficult to get this precious commodity through to a chemically dependent person. Addicts, secretly despising themselves, are likely to respond to another person who approaches them in a loving manner by wondering what this person wants, assuming that the person is a "sucker" ripe for manipulation, or deciding that the person is crazy. In this way, they fail to receive the praise, warmth, and tenderness they crave, and instead wind up lashing out at those who try to love them.

In treatment, the trick is to somehow break through the barriers that alcoholics and addicts erect against receiving love and acceptance, to help them learn to love and accept themselves. One way to begin to accomplish this task is to view their low self-esteem as a *hunger* for love and acceptance, and therefore as a motive. A motive is something that can be used. Experimental psychologists do much the same thing when they define their laboratory animals as hungry if they have been deprived of food for a given period of time. The next step is to think about ways that love and acceptance could be made palatable, or how they might be packaged so that alcoholics and addicts will let them "in."

One way for a therapist to "sneak" the love in is to let patients know that he or she *understands*. The easiest way to do that is to be an alcoholic or addict oneself, and to disclose some of the details of one's addiction and recovery to one's patients. Even though a

therapist is a recovering alcoholic or addict, some patients will
resist the therapist's positive regard, because they construe the
therapist as having sold out, as being an authority figure, or as
not really caring because he or she is being paid to care.
Therefore, although having had the experience of addiction oneself is helpful, it is often not enough. A therapist must have many
different skills, the possession of which can allow even nonaddicted, nonrecovering therapists to be effective with chemically
dependent patients.

Another way to show that one understands is to face and talk
frankly about the reality of the disease and the patient's expected
reactions to anyone who might try to help. By naming the resist-
ances that the patient is likely to use, before he or she uses them,
the therapist can prevent the patient from employing them. At the
same time, the therapist can demonstrate an understanding of the
secret, lonely desperation of addiction by describing how he or she
thinks the patient might feel about life, about recovery, and about
therapists. Once a therapist has had adequate experience in working with and listening to recovering chemically dependent
patients, he or she will be able to describe fairly accurately the
patient's pain, hopelessness, lack of trust, and other feelings.
A patient whose pain and self-loathing have been accurately
described by a therapist is more likely to allow him- or herself to
experience the therapist's loving and caring feelings, and then to
begin to experience a measure of self-love.

Erickson had a way of talking with alcoholics and others that
let them know instantly that he understood the self-esteem issue,
even though he was not chemically dependent. For example, an
alcoholic patient who had been very well known came to Erickson
with a scrapbook filled with news clippings and aviation records
from his past to show that there was "something good" in him,
that he was "worth salvaging" (Haley, 1985). He emphasized to
Erickson that he was willing to do anything and that he trusted
Erickson to "talk straight" to him. Erickson agreed that he would
work with him, but in his own way.

Erickson's way was to accuse the man of coming in under false pretenses, and to call the man a "dirty, filthy, foul-smelling, unshaven bum" who had no right to carry a respectable man's scrapbook with him. Erickson continued with his "diatribe" for an hour and a half, then dismissed the man, predicting that he would get drunk right away.

The man returned a few months later, and Erickson asked him if he really wanted to enter therapy. When the man said that he did, Erickson told him that the "dressing down" he had given him before was "just an introduction," and that this time he was really going to tell him what he was. This time, he denounced the man for three hours.

The man responded by joining a gymnasium and getting into good physical shape. Then he joined the Air Corps and was commissioned a Captain. Later he rose to Major and Lieutenant Colonel and was sent to the Pentagon. In the meantime, a couple of months after the three-hour visit, he called Erickson and said that he felt like drinking. Erickson told him to bring the bottle over, and he (Erickson) would supply the glasses and ice. When the man arrived, Erickson offered to match him drink for drink, until they were drunk together. The man refused the offer and left. He stayed sober from that point, as far as Erickson knew.

How did the "hour and a half of diatribe and that three hours of vituperation" help the man, who obviously already had very low self-esteem? The man had asked Erickson to be straight with him. If Erickson had done anything other than denounce him, the man would have known that Erickson was not being straight with him. Erickson not only let him have it, he let him have it lavishly and without restraint. The man's low self esteem was a bar against receiving any expression of love or concern. Erickson was not rebuffed by this obstacle. He used it. He spoke in the harshest and most derogatory terms possible, thereby making it impossible for the man to assume that he was offering phony concern. Yet he demonstrated concern anyway. He showed respect by letting the man know that he believed the man could take it if he were told the whole truth. The respect was a message of caring that the man could not resist. That caring, coupled with the hard confrontation of reality, got the man's attention. Then, Erickson's prediction of relapse utilized the man's predictable anger and defiance, while his offer to "sacrifice" his own sobriety helped the man get through a crisis.

Another example is of an obese 21-year-old woman (Haley, 1973), who told Erickson on the telephone before meeting him that she was sure he would not want to see her, and who then tried to leave his office even before sitting down at her first appointment, feeling convinced that she had been right. Recognizing that her self-esteem was extremely low, Erickson decided that he would have to talk to her with "unkindness and brutality," in order to "convince her of my sincerity." He concluded that she would "misinterpret any kindness and could not possibly believe courteous language."

Erickson briefly took her history and then asked her height and weight. She told him and added that she was "just a plain, fat slob," and that nobody would ever look at her "except with disgust." He responded by telling her that she had failed to tell him the truth. He pointed out that she was not a *plain*, fat, disgusting slob, but the "fattest, homeliest, most disgustingly horrible bucket of lard" he had ever seen. He continued with his assessment, describing in detail her nose that was "mashed" onto her face, her crooked teeth, her uncombed hair, her dress with "millions and billions" of polka dots, and so on. Then he asked her why she had come to see him. She replied that she hoped he could hypnotize her to help her lose weight. Using a direct, authoritarian approach, he did hypnotize her and proceeded with the therapy, which eventually proved to be quite successful.

Erickson recognized that he would lose the woman as a patient unless he met the resistance caused by her low self-esteem head-on. In doing so, he appeared to be esteeming her as lowly as she esteemed herself, which must have been a relief for her. She probably welcomed his negative assessment of her, because he was willing to meet and work with her in spite of her appearance, and she did not have to wait in suspense for him to reject her because of it. In short, by talking to her the way he did, Erickson made her poor self-image work for the therapy instead of undermining it.

Therapists should never pretend or manufacture loving, caring feelings about their chemically dependent patients. The patients will sniff out the therapist's deception instantaneously. Therapists should also be careful about expressing genuine loving concern right away. Patients will suspect and reject it if the therapist expresses it too soon to be believable, or too soon for them to feel that they earned it. One way for therapists to let patients know that they love them, in addition to the technique of bluntly pointing out their flaws, as Erickson did (and which could easily backfire unless practiced with utmost care), is to let them know that they hate their disease. Great headway can be made by therapists who describe the disease of addiction in strongly emotional terms, leaving the unstated implication that they care about and advocate the needs of the victims of this odious illness.

Perhaps the best way to ensure that chemically dependent patients accept and incorporate the love and concern of others is to promote loving and caring interactions among them in groups, and encourage them to spend time with other people whose love and concern they can accept. Group therapy is the staple of inpatient and residential treatment settings, and for most outpatient programs, and that makes them ideal settings to create a loving atmosphere among peers. An individual therapist, who is not part of a program, can harness peer acceptance by putting his or her chemically dependent patients together in groups, if there are enough of them. If not, the very best option is to encourage, or, better yet, require, participation in Alcoholics Anonymous and similar groups (such as Narcotics Anonymous, Cocaine Anonymous, etc.). In fact, A.A. should be required even if patients are attending group therapy.

Patients will readily see that their peers in groups and in A.A. can give them the love and acceptance they hunger for, and they will realize that they have no alternative but to accept it, because it is freely given from one addict or alcoholic to another with no strings attached. In this way, their low self-esteem—their hunger for love and acceptance—works for them, to "hook" them strongly into a system of recovering people. The key is to introduce peer groups and A.A. properly to new patients, so that they will discover that the love and concern available from members of these groups is genuine, is not part of a manipulation, and—especially with A.A.—is given not out of a desire to do good, but out of the belief that helping another alcoholic or addict is the best way to help oneself.

UTILIZING PAIN

Pain and its avoidance or escape is a primary motivator in chemical dependency. In fact, it may well be *the* primary motivator. Pain also has a more positive effect: under appropriate circumstances, it motivates people to seek recovery. Generally, an addict or alcoholic will seek treatment when the pain caused by the addiction is greater than the pain relief provided by the substance to which he or she is addicted. Chemically dependent people find the thought of living without their chemicals to be frightening indeed. Yet, as threatening as treatment and recovery are for addicts and alcoholics, they come in for treatment, and there is no shortage of them. The fact that they are there is a testament to the power of pain as a motivator.

A well-planned intervention utilizes pain by communicating to the chemically dependent person the true extent of the consequences of his or her chemical use. Once the person's defenses are down, although it is only for a short time, the person becomes capable of feeling the pain that he or she is in (all the pain—besides just the guilt, which was described earlier in this chapter in connection with interventions). Suddenly, the person is motivated to seek recovery.

Is It Bad Enough Yet?

A therapist can use pain to therapeutic advantage by considering the relentlessly progressive quality of addiction and the inevitability of ever-mounting pain, and then making that promise of pain the patient's problem and not the therapist's. When the patient shows resistance to treatment or fails to follow therapeutic directions as if his or her life depends on it (which it does), the therapist can tell the patient something like the following:

> You're probably expecting me to do something to try to get you motivated—maybe chew you out, or make some bleeding heart plea, like asking you to think about all you have to live for or the people you'll hurt. Well, you can forget that. I know I don't have to do anything to motivate you. I know that you have the disease of addiction, that you'll have it for the rest of your life, and that it will always get worse, never better. I don't have to motivate you, because your disease will. It'll motivate you with *pain.*
>
> You seem to have forgotten about the pain of your disease: the "pitiful and incomprehensible demoralization;" the pain that's so bad, everything seems to hurt, even your hair. You're acting like you think it will never come back. But don't worry, it will. If you don't believe me, just go out now and take a drink or use a drug. And don't waste any time. Do it right away—today! And when you do, the pain will come back. Maybe not right away, but it'll come back, and this time it will be even worse.
>
> I know I can't stop you if you want to drink or use. I don't have to. And I have no interest in punishing you for it if you do. Your disease will punish you. And it will do a better job of punishing you than I ever could. It's a powerful thing, and I have confidence in it. It hasn't disappointed me yet. I don't have to do anything; your disease will do it all. I'll just ask you if it's bad enough yet.

Once a therapist has delivered this speech, or one like it, he or she can simply ask: "Is it bad enough yet?" or state: "It sounds like it's not bad enough yet," any time in the future that patients who have not followed therapeutic directions to the letter complain of some discomfort in their lives. Eventually, they are bound to get the message.

UTILIZING THE NEED FOR EXCITEMENT

Many addicts are sensation seekers or have a strong need for excitement. This tendency keeps them living "on the edge," taking risks and creating high drama in their relationships with other people. When sensation seekers and excitement junkies contemplate lives of sobriety, they are bound to find the prospect boring beyond belief—and boredom is extremely painful to such a person. If a therapist wants to help such patients, he or she must overcome or utilize this obstacle. Overcoming it is nearly impossible, because a sensation seeker will simply leave or turn away from a boring experience. Utilization is a much more effective and practical approach.

One way to utilize a patient's need for excitement is to make the treatment experience exciting and dramatic. Many alcoholics and addicts derive great pleasure from recounting and embellishing their drinking and drug-using escapades (accounts which are often referred to as "drunk-a-logues"). Why not help create for them a set of recovery memories that equal their drinking and drug-using memories in drama and excitement? Patients are more likely to stay "hooked" into treatment if therapists and counselors make a consistent effort to "spice up" the treatment experience and keep it interesting even to patients who are accustomed to a high level of stimulation in their lives prior to entering treatment.

Making treatment exciting is a more manageable task in an inpatient program or therapeutic community, since therapists or program directors can design the overall environment in these settings. The next chapter describes some methods used that can create excitement and drama in groups. Therapists can add these qualities to outpatient settings or private practices, but they need much energy and imagination to do it. For example, it is no accident that therapists and counselors who work successfully with chemically dependent

patients are often rather flamboyant when compared with mental
health (only) therapists. They often dress, speak, and carry themselves in ways that make them seem "larger than life." They are ora-
tors rather than lecturers, and they often employ powerful,
emotional approaches and behave in dramatic and unpredictable
ways in their clinical work. They have "magnetic" personalities, and
often attract followings. Their former patients or clients enjoy telling
stories about them. In short, they are adept at utilizing their patients'
and clients' need for excitement.

Utilizing "Convict Honor"

One of Erickson's therapy stories involved his utilization of an
alcoholic's convict honor (Personal Communication, 1978):

> An alcoholic who was down on his luck, out of money, and
> without a place to stay, walked many miles in the hot desert
> sun to Erickson's house and asked Erickson to tell him what
> to do to get sober. Erickson did tell him, and after he was
> through, the alcoholic said: "You know where you can shove
> that!" and stormed out to drink some more. By and by, he
> returned, again traveling miles by foot through the heat of
> Phoenix to get there, and asked Erickson to repeat what he
> had told him before. Erickson did, and when he was done,
> the man said: "You know where you can shove that!" and
> walked out again.
>
> Surprisingly, the man appeared a third time, once again
> asking Erickson to repeat what he had told him the other two
> times. Erickson replied that he could not do so, because he
> had "shoved it," but instead offered the man his backyard
> as a place to stay while putting his life back together. To
> insure that the man would stay, he made an offer based on
> his knowledge of convict honor, which he had acquired while
> working in prisons, and which he employed because he knew
> that the man had once been a convict. He offered to take the

man's boots, if the man wanted him to, so that he would be unable to leave the backyard. When the man respectfully declined the offer, Erickson knew that he would stay, because convict honor dictated it. Years later, the man frequently spoke in A.A. meetings about his "backyard launching pad."

CONFUSION

Confusion is an inevitable part of both addiction and recovery. Addiction creates confusion because of the powerful ability of alcohol and drugs to alter perception, emotion, and thinking, which creates a gap in the addicted person's mind between what is real and what is not, both internally and in the external world. Addicts and alcoholics respond to the confusion by acting as if they are not confused, as if they are aware, certain, and in control. They hate internal confusion, and they go to great lengths to defend against it, and yet they constantly create it.

Recovery generates confusion, because it forces addicted people both to become aware of the confusion that they have been denying and to allow and experience new confusion. The new confusion occurs as the result of changing, or being changed, at deep, unconscious, structural levels of the self.

CONFUSION-RESTRUCTURING

The concept of confusion-restructuring (originally developed by Erickson, Rossi, & Rossi, 1976) has two meanings here: First, it describes the process of deep, unconscious change that accompanies recovery, and second, it describes hypnosis and therapy techniques which are actually methods of utilizing confusion. Both meanings of the concept are explored below.

The first meaning of the term confusion-restructuring has to do with the change process that takes place deep in the unconscious mind of addicts and alcoholics as they recover, which was addressed in the previous chapter, in the discussion of surrender. The script below is often used with patients to describe the process of recovery. Giving patients this description, while encouraging them to welcome confusion, is one way to facilitate the confusion-restructuring process in them. This script should be modified to suit the therapist's style and the patient's level of understanding, and may be given with the patient in or out of trance:

During your recovery, you are likely to experience a great deal of *confusion*. Most people hate feeling confused, but you'll need to learn to welcome it. That's because confusion is a beautiful thing. Here's why:

A person's mind, point of view, or orientation to life jells or crystallizes, then becomes fairly permanent. If it is a "good" or adequate frame of reference, point of view, or atti-tude, it will be adaptive and reflect reality fairly accurately. However, time and situations change; people's perspectives change with age; and eventually, no matter how effective a person's frame of reference may have been at one time, it will eventually become outmoded and will need to change.

One approach to this situation is to simply tack on amend-ments, to leave the original crystallization intact, and to add on superficial modifications here and there. However, there comes a time when this approach no longer works and the entire structure needs to dissolve and be replaced by a crystal with a different structure that more adequately reflects the current reality.

When the old frame of reference dissolves and is replaced by a new one, the person undergoing the experience feels a very profound sense of confusion. It is as if, while the old frame of reference is dissolved and the new one has yet to be constructed, there is *no* frame of reference. The person has no familiar way of assessing reality. During that time, the per-son is subject to a great deal of fear and confusion. You need to remember, when this happens to you, that the confusion is not part of the problem. It is part of the solution. It is not sickness or "craziness." It is health. You'll be *"going sane."*

One way to tailor this description to the patient, besides adjusting the vocabulary level and grammar, is to add analogies to which the patient can relate. For example, if the patient is familiar with automobile engines, the therapist can compare the difference between superficial and deep change with the difference between adjusting a carburetor and rebuilding the engine. When the engine is in bad enough condition, just turning a screw to adjust the carburetor is not enough. Major repairs are needed. The period of confusion, in which there is no clear frame of reference, can be compared to having the engine apart, with pistons over here, valves over there, and nothing to power the car. The new frame of reference can be likened to a re-engineered, rebuilt, and vastly improved engine.

The other meaning of the term confusion-restructuring refers to a set of therapeutic techniques, which Erickson and co-authors called the confusion-restructuring approach (Erickson, Rossi, & Rossi, 1976). Use of these techniques begins with an understanding that confused people have a strong need for clarifying information. Confusion is a state in which people temporarily lose the sense of certainty and confidence that characterizes their routine orientation to the environment. Their usual frames of reference are "unstructured," and they are off balance and at a loss as to what to do next. Therefore, they need and will actively seek and apply any information that looks like it will be able to reduce their disorientation and restore their sense of knowing what to do—that is, "restructure" their frames of reference. This need makes confused people particularly susceptible to hypnotic or therapeutic suggestions, especially when the suggestions are given by a therapist who understands how to induce and/or utilize confusion.

An example of Erickson's induction and utilization of confusion occurred with a patient who had failed to be hypnotized by several different doctors after many of hours of trying (Erickson, 1967).

Erickson recognized immediately that the patient wanted therapy but was resistant, and that she would embroil him in a contest of wills if he were to use a direct approach. Therefore, after she told him that he would probably also fail to hypnotize her, he told her that he expected resistance from her. Then, with a completely different tone of voice and tempo, he stated: "I CAN'T HYPNOTIZE YOU, justyourarm." When she expressed bewilderment and asked what he meant, he slowly and emphatically stated: "THAT'S EXACTLY WHAT I MEAN. I CAN'T HYPNOTIZE YOU" . . . "justyourarm, see." And with that, he gently guided her arm upward, where it remained suspended cataleptically. She was in a somnambulistic trance.

Erickson had created a brief moment of confusion by his dramatically different tone of voice and emphasis, and by his odd remark about hypnotizing, not her, but just her arm. He resolved this confusion by offering a nonverbal suggestion, which consisted of guiding her arm upward. That slight touch contained the crucial piece of information which she could use to solve the puzzle he created by his apparently nonsensical behavior. The only hitch was that she had to go into a trance in order to apply this clarifying information.

If one wants to facilitate confusion, it is useful to "pepper" one's therapeutic communication with statements that surprise or startle patients and force them to become open to new information and different ways of looking at things. Erickson was a master of such statements. An example of his ability to shock patients was given above, and others were described earlier in the stories of his treatment of the alcoholic man and the obese woman. He accused both of them of being dishonest with him—the man, for pretending to be a respectable, successful person, and the woman, for calling herself a "plain" fat slob. These accusations most certainly evoked momentary disorientation in both patients and secured their undivided attention.

Another intervention, aimed at creating shock and momentary disorientation, is often useful with patients who are in denial of their addictions. It consists of the therapist telling them: "I don't know if you are an alcoholic (or addict, etc.—as applicable), but I *hope* you are." The therapist then goes on to list the things that he or she hopes the patient is *not*, but could very well be, judging from the patient's past behavior and current situation, such as a liar, a cheat, a philanderer, a psychopath, a criminal, an immoral low-life, just plain crazy, etc. The therapist explains that "Something is wrong. Something is causing this behavior and these problems. Out of all the things it *could* be, I hope it is chemical dependency."

USEFUL AND HARMFUL CONFUSION

All the foregoing statements about confusion must be tempered by the knowledge that confusion should be used judiciously. A therapist should never confuse patients for the sake of confusion alone. There are times when patients need to be confused, and there are times when they need to feel clear-minded and certain— especially chemically dependent patients. Judging when to confuse and when to clarify is a primary task for any therapist or counselor who uses confusion therapeutically with addicts and alcoholics.

Often, there is a relationship between subjects about which a therapist confuses and clarifies. For example, an astute therapist should confuse patients' assumptions about their own addictions, and about addiction in general, when those patients are in denial or delusion about the fact that they are addicted, and when they have faulty information about the nature of the disease. While the patient is confused, the therapist should insert new and accurate information about these issues, with confidence that the patient will accept it because of the increased need for clarifying information generated by the confusion.

Therapists and counselors need to be crystal clear whenever they communicate with patients about *solutions*—that is, when stating philosophical principles of recovery (such as A.A. or other therapeutic concepts), and when giving directions about how to carry out therapeutic tasks and assignments. The risk is too great that some patients, particularly those in early recovery, will be lost in a boozy or drugged-out fog and thus unable to understand or remember crucial information. Not only should therapists communicate clearly about these things, they should repeat them often—far more often than they would to an ordinary audience, and what may seem to be *ad nauseum* to therapists accustomed to working with more clearheaded patients. It is not unusual for addicted patients to comment after "n" repetitions of some crucial point that they just heard it for the first time.

STRATEGIC PLANNING

Erickson's work has often been described as planful or strategic (i.e., by Haley, 1973), because he typically directed and coordinated the therapeutic process, in either a direct and obvious or an indirect and mysterious manner. He seemed to assume that therapists should not leave it up to sick and misguided patients to determine the course of their treatment. This assumption is, without doubt, the best starting point in working with addicted patients, because so many of them are deluded about their addictions and can be expected to act on the basis of their delusions instead of in their own long-term self-interest. In other words, addicted patients often need to be "tricked" into recovery. One way to do that is to strategically plan an approach to their treatment and carry out the plan without revealing it to them.

The following case is an example of strategic planning that was employed with a man who was referred for treatment after his second arrest for drunk driving.

Hank was angry at the policeman who had cited him, feeling that the officer had been waiting outside the bar, "like a vulture," to trap the next person who came out. Hank had been unfortunate enough (as he saw it) to be the next one out, and was thus, in his mind, a helpless, innocent victim. He clung to this myth of the unfairness of his arrest instead of looking at the fact that he had been drunk and was doubtless an unsafe driver. This issue preoccupied him and kept his focus on the police officer instead of on himself and whether he was an alcoholic. The therapist's task was to break through this thinking and help Hank to consider objectively the question of his addiction.

Hank was seeing the therapist with the understanding that the therapist would document his cooperation and participation, and that the judge would see the documentation at the time of sentencing. He was hoping that the judge would take this evidence of his sincerity into account and possibly give him a lighter sentence, so he was strongly "motivated" to cooperate. Arranging in advance the possibility of this payoff for Hank, and his resultant motivation to cooperate, is the first stage of the strategy.

The therapist elicited a history which revealed, among other things, that Hank believed himself not to be alcoholic at all. The therapist pointed out that he had no opinion on whether Hank was or was not an alcoholic, but he added that it was an important question because of the seriousness of the disease. He told Hank that if Hank had a suspicious lump, it might be a symptom of cancer, and Hank ought to see a doctor immediately to find out whether or not the lump was cancerous. The therapist explained that alcoholism was a terminal disease and was just as serious and deadly as cancer, and that Hank's drunk-driving arrest was his "lump," that is, a symptom which suggested the possibility of alcoholism. He then offered to take a thorough look, together with Hank, at all the evidence for and against the diagnosis of alcoholism. The second stage of the strategy, then, was to structure the interaction as a health-focused, rather than a legalistic or punishment-oriented one, and to define the goal as joint, open-minded exploration rather than finger-pointing and accusation with moral overtones.

The therapist pointed out the difficulty of diagnosing alcoholism by bringing up the fact that one of the most serious symptoms of alcoholism is the belief that one does not have it. Therefore, the therapist exclaimed, when a patient says that he is not alcoholic, it means either that he is or that he is not. This was the third stage of the strategy, which was to create doubt and confusion in Hank's mind about the validity of Hank's assertion that he was not alcoholic.

The therapist then stated that, since they were not sure if Hank was alcoholic, but there was reason to believe that he might be, it was therefore important for Hank's health and safety that he follow sound clinical advice and not drink any alcohol or use any drugs during the course of the treatment. The therapist added that, if Hank *was* alcoholic, then avoiding alcohol and drugs would prevent the disease from advancing, and if Hank was *not* alcoholic, then avoiding alcohol and drugs would prevent him from *becoming* alcoholic. In either case, it was a prudent course of behavior. By showing Hank the wisdom of avoiding alcohol, regardless of whether or not Hank was alcoholic, the therapist was able to address the issue of abstinence independently of the question of whether or not Hank was alcoholic, thereby avoiding any resistance Hank may have mounted to abstaining because "Why should I if I'm not an alcoholic?"

Then, the therapist asked Hank to make a formal commitment to avoid all alcohol and drugs during treatment, but to *let the therapist know if he did* drink or use drugs. The therapist assured Hank that there would be no judgments or accusations if Hank drank or used, but that he needed to be fully informed of any drinking or using that Hank might do, if he was to be of any help to Hank. Before Hank had time to answer, the therapist casually observed that sometimes patients had difficulty making this commitment, and that their difficulty was, in fact, evidence that they were alcoholic, since only alcoholics would find such a commitment difficult, while nonalcoholics would find it no more difficult to avoid alcohol than to avoid, say, broccoli.

The therapist ensured that Hank would make the commitment by allowing Hank to report any drinking he might do in spite of his commitment, because the alcoholic mind, which would fear total deprivation from alcohol, was more likely to go along with a commitment to abstain knowing that there was a possible loophole in it. Hank's "alcoholic honor"— similar to the "convict honor" that Erickson counted on in an example given earlier—ensured that Hank would live up to the contract by reporting his drinking or drug use if he did drink or use drugs. The therapist put in place additional assurance of compliance by implying that a failure by Hank to comply would prove his alcoholism. Hank had to agree in order not to admit his alcoholism.

The fourth stage of the strategy was in place. The therapist had gotten Hank to agree not to drink or use, and to tell him if he did. It is often a sound strategy to ask an addicted patient to make a commitment which seems innocent or simple at the time, but which has powerful implications that the patient does not foresee. The commitment that Hank made had extremely potent and far-reaching implications. Hank now had two options with regard to drinking or using: to do so or not. In either case, he was already committed to a course of action that would undermine his denial and encourage recovery.

If Hank did *not* drink or use, he would have a clear head and thus be able to fully participate in treatment with the therapist, to listen to other alcoholics with whom he might identify, to attend A.A. meetings and read A.A. literature, and to complete written homework on both. During this treatment, assuming he stayed clean and sober through it, he had a maximal chance of breaking through his delusion, identifying himself as alcoholic and continuing his recovery.

If Hank *did* drink or use, and if he told the therapist about it as promised, he would soon find himself facing some hard questions. (Perhaps surprisingly, many patients treated this way *have* reported drinking or drug use, indicating that patients asked to make this commitment in the way described above did tend to openly admit their alcohol or drug use.) The therapist would take his report of drinking or using as an important piece of data, and would explore with Hank what his failure to keep the commitment meant. Did it mean that he was completely irresponsible and incapable of keeping commitments?

Did the failure mean that all along Hank had never meant to keep his commitment and was therefore a liar? Did it mean that he was completely out of control of his behavior and therefore mentally ill? Or did it mean that he was alcoholic? When considering these options, the therapist would say: "I hope you are an alcoholic" (instead of irresponsible, a liar, or crazy), as described above in the section on confusion.

What actually happened in this case was that Hank did drink and told the therapist about it. "But I only had one beer," he proclaimed proudly, and the therapist's questions about the meaning of the drinking failed to make a dent in his denial. However, the next week, Hank reported drinking again, and this time he had "only two" beers. The third week, he reported having "only three" beers. Each time, Hank maintained that he was in control of his drinking, and that the small number of beers he had had was proof of his control. The therapist finally replied that it seemed to him that Hank was in control all right, but each week he was in control of a larger amount of beer. If he kept this up, he would soon be in control of a keg a day. The fifth week, Hank reported that he had lost control and had a binge, and he asked to be hospitalized for treatment. On last contact, Hank was maintaining good sobriety.

USE OF TRANCE

Hypnosis has been offered as a cure for just about every "bad habit" that humans are heir to, including nailbiting, bedwetting, cigarette smoking, overeating, and poor study habits. Following in this long tradition, one might be tempted to view alcoholism and drug addiction as similar bad habits and attempt to cure them with hypnosis. This notion gives rise to an earnest caveat: Addiction is a complex, multifaceted disease, not simply a habit, and therefore one would have to be either a complete neophyte or an irresponsible quack to attempt to treat it only with hypnosis. To offer hypnosis alone—or any solitary, elementary approach, for that matter (for example, disulfiram alone)—and either state or imply that it by itself is sufficient to bring about recovery would be maltreatment of the worst sort. It would clearly validate the need or desire so often seen in addicted patients to appear to be doing something about their addiction while actually avoiding any real change. (Please note that some of the "bad habits" mentioned above also are or can be complex, addictive diseases and should not be treated with hypnosis alone either; that includes many cases of cigarette smoking, which are often actually nicotine addiction, and overeating, which may be a symptom of an eating disorder.)

There are uses for hypnosis, however, within the context of an overall, comprehensive treatment approach. Habits, both of behavior and of thought, do comprise a portion of the addictive problem, and hypnosis aimed at changing these habits can be useful as an adjunct to the therapeutic effort. Teaching patients to relax without alcohol or drugs is another legitimate adjunctive use of hypnosis.

Of course, these applications of hypnosis make sense only if the patient is actually interested in recovery. Because of the nature of addiction, a counselor or therapist can never be sure that a given patient really wants to change habits or learn to relax without chemicals. The patient may be just complying superficially. Superficially compliant patients will go along with whatever treatment they are offered, but they engage in game-playing that can turn any treatment, no matter how carefully conceived or earnestly given, into a meaningless exercise or laughable travesty.

To avoid these games, therapists and treatment programs should direct the main thrust of their energy toward smashing compliance and facilitating surrender. Once a patient has surrendered, he or she will not only be open to, but will actively seek, any and all approaches that show even the remotest chance of being able to advance recovery.

In spite of these warnings, there are some very powerful applications for hypnosis in treatment of chemically dependent persons. For example, in addition to the uses briefly mentioned above, hypnosis can be very useful as a metaphor for surrender and for helping patients to conceptualize a relationship with a Higher Power. It can also be translated into Twelve-Step terminology and taught as a form of meditation. Below is a script for teaching meditation in this way.

> You may not realize it, but you have *two* minds: a conscious mind and an unconscious mind. In case you have difficulty believing that you have an unconscious mind, let me point out an example of how it works. Remember the last time you tried hard to remember something, like the name of an actor on the late show on TV. "What's his name? What's his name?" you may have asked yourself over and over. And then, not coming up with an answer, you probably gave up. Later, maybe in a few minutes or a half hour, or maybe a day or more later, the answer came to you. It just popped into your mind while you were thinking about something else entirely. Have you had an experience like that? (*Patients invariably say that they have, and often enjoy recounting the experience.*)
>
> This kind of experience is evidence that there are mental processes going on in your mind that you are unaware of consciously. While you were occupied with an unrelated train of conscious thought, your unconscious mind was searching its memory banks, comparing mental pictures of old actors with its stores of actors' names, until it finally came up with a match and then delivered the answer to your conscious mind by "popping" it into your awareness.
>
> Here's another example of unconscious processing. Many people have this experience, and maybe you have had it too.

Have you ever had a very important reason to get up at a certain time in the morning, set your alarm for that time, and then found yourself waking up just before the alarm was set to go off? [*Patients invariably report that they have.*] This is another example of a function that your unconscious mind can perform for you. You know that your unconscious mind did it, because you weren't awake counting the minutes and seconds, or watching the clock. You were asleep and unconscious. But while you slept, your unconscious mind was keeping perfect time for you and then wakened you with uncanny accuracy.

Let me tell you a little more about your unconscious mind. While I am talking to you, everything I say is being recorded for permanent storage in your mind. So is every voice inflection and emphasis, every facial expression, the clothes I am wearing, where I am sitting, where you are sitting, the pictures on the wall, the sounds outside the office, the room temperature, any smells, other sensory input, and the thoughts and associations running through your mind as I talk. All that is being recorded now, and your mind is recording that kind of information all the time. When you stop to think about the sheer volume of information that is stored in your mind, you will soon realize that it is immense. There must be as much information stored in your mind as there is in all the libraries in the world. If I am exaggerating, it isn't by very much.

If your mind contains that much information, it also needs a way to manage it. Libraries have complex systems for storing and retrieving information, and you would need a masters degree in library science to fully comprehend them. Computers also have systems, called disk operating systems, that handle storage, retrieval, and other information management functions. These systems are also very complicated and most computer users who are able to work with them still do not understand all the intricacies of how they work.

Your mind also has an information management system.

But it is different from the systems used in libraries and in computers, because the volume of information that your mind handles and the number of levels on which it functions simultaneously are so much greater. This system is very complex. In fact, it is too complex for you to keep up with or even begin to understand consciously. It just works quietly in the background, taking care of many, many functions automatically and providing your conscious mind with the information it needs as you consciously make information requests and allow yourself to be receptive to its offerings.

Consider some of the functions your unconscious mind takes care of automatically: Try to stand up and walk consciously. Can you do it? Of course not. To consciously control this simple behavior, you would need to know which muscle to move first, then next, and so forth, and how much to contract each muscle, and whether and how much to relax opposing muscles, and how to communicate with and command each muscle individually and choreograph "harmonies" and "chords" of movements of groups of muscles, and monitor input from the inner ear in order to make minute compensations to maintain balance, and a host of other tasks that would overwhelm your conscious mind if you even begin to try to manage this behavior consciously. What you do consciously is have the thought that you want to stand up and walk over there, and then your unconscious mind takes over and makes it possible.

Another behavior that you probably think you control consciously—but don't—is talking. To control talking consciously, you would have to formulate an idea of what ideas you want to convey, then go to your word storage bins and select out the words you want from the millions of words there (including foreign languages if you know any, baby talk and other words that you don't use anymore, and profanity, which may or may not be appropriate with the person you are talking to). Then, you would have to string the words together in a meaningful way, punctuate them, add emphasis, add facial expressions and hand and body movements, and then control the muscles of the voice box, diaphragm, mouth and tongue, and others—and do all that in a fraction of a second.

You can't possibly do all that consciously. In fact, what you do consciously is a much more limited function. You become aware of what you are about to say an instant before it comes out, so that you can do a last minute edit job to catch little errors and eliminate them before anyone can hear them.

Another thing your conscious mind does is believe that it is consciously in control of everything you are doing. When you stop to consider all the things you would have to do in order to be in conscious control, however, you will soon realize that you are not in conscious control of very much at all. Yet your conscious mind will probably continue to believe that it knows all and controls all. That stubborn illusion is at the root of many of our problems. It leads us to try to exert conscious control over problems and tasks that are way beyond the capacity of our conscious minds. In most of these efforts, we fail miserably until we give up and let the smart part of us take over.

The smart part of us is our creative unconscious mind. It is the part that is always listening, pondering, associating, and watching over us as we consciously fumble our way through life. It is the part that knows much more than we do and is willing to tell us if we will only ask. It is the part that has already formulated several alternative solutions to each of our problems, complete with the capacity to adjust as contingencies change. It is extremely powerful and creative. It creates one or more Oscar-quality movies—dreams— every night and plays them for us while we sleep. In Hollywood, it takes hundreds of people, tens of millions of dollars, and several months to make just one. The creative unconscious mind is the source of all of our creative ideas and inspirations. In short, it is a *power greater than our conscious selves.*

How do most of us relate to our own creative unconscious mind, this power greater than our conscious selves? We boss it around, insisting that it do things our way—our conscious and limited way. It is like the tail trying to wag the dog. We trust it to help us walk or to keep our hearts beating, but when faced with complex life problems, we shun its suggestions, which it generally offers in subtle and gentle ways, and ask it for help only after we have exhausted ourselves and proven our consciously derived solutions to be dismal failures. What does our creative unconscious mind do when we insist on handling things consciously? In most cases it lets us. Like a wise and patient parent, it lets us. And even though we may have ignored it for years, it is ready with solutions for us immediately as soon as we become willing to consult it, trust it, and rely on it.

Let's look at some of the Twelve Steps and see where our creative unconscious minds fit in. Step Two states: "Came to believe that a Power greater than ourselves could restore us to sanity." If we change the word "ourselves" to "our conscious selves," the meaning stays essentially the same, but illustrates how it is possible to conceive of this Power as being our creative unconscious mind.

Step Three states: "Made a decision to turn our will and our lives over to the care of God *as we understood Him*." With no offense meant to anyone who believes in God (but with potential benefit to anyone who cannot for the time being handle the concept of a religious God), suppose we decide to understand God by thinking of Him as our creative unconscious minds? When we do so, we understand this step as a suggestion that we turn our conscious will and all decisions about how to solve the problems in our lives over to the care of our creative unconscious minds.

Finally, let's look at Step Eleven: "Sought through prayer and meditation to improve our conscious contact with God *as we understood Him*, praying only for knowledge of his will for us and the power to carry that out." With our present understanding, we can read this step as a method whereby we seek to "improve our conscious contact with our creative unconscious mind, praying only for knowledge of its will for us and the power to carry that out."

Steps Two, Three, and Eleven, then, are very clear suggestions that we stop trying to run our lives based on the illusion that we are in conscious control, and instead let the smart part of our minds—our creative unconscious minds—take over that job. When we come to believe that this approach will help (Step Two), decide to try it (Step Three), and then strive to maintain that stance by improving our conscious contact through prayer and meditation (Step Eleven), our creative unconscious mind will restore us to sanity and can then have broader and more far-reaching applications by solving problems "in all our affairs" (as Step Twelve states).

When viewed from this perspective, the essence of the Twelve Steps is that we reverse the usual relationship of conscious to unconscious minds: We stop trying to make the creative unconscious mind conform to our conscious desires; instead, we surrender conscious control and allow our unconscious mind to be the boss.

This is where meditation comes in. It is a method that we can practice regularly to make it easier for our conscious mind to turn over control to our creative unconscious mind. It is like letting our unconscious mind "out to play," without monitoring or interfering with the free play of the unconscious, inspirational process. Since our unconscious mind almost always, without hesitating, allows our conscious mind to interrupt and take back control, the meditation technique we choose should be designed to keep our conscious mind occupied, so that it is as unlikely as possible to continue to interfere, as is its usual habit to do.

Occupying the conscious mind so that it is less likely to interfere is the essence of meditation. Most meditation techniques are based on engaging in some kind of thought in a repetitive way that keeps the conscious mind harmlessly busy, bored, or distracted, and allows the unconscious mind free creative rein.

For example, one technique consists of thinking a word or a sound called a mantra—which in some techniques is a Sanscrit word and therefore meaningless to us—over and over, rhythmically. This process has the effect of boring the conscious mind and moving it harmlessly out of the way. A more Western version of this same technique is to think a familiar word over and over, such as the word "One" or "Relax" or "Love" or "Peace." It really doesn't matter which word or sound you think, as long as you are comfortable with it and it has the intended effect. When you think it, you can just repeat it slowly or you can tie it in with the rhythm of your breathing—whatever feels most comfortable.

The repeating word or mantra technique is based on using one form of imagery: auditory or sound imagery. Another way to meditate with auditory imagery is to hear or play music in your mind. If you choose that, it would be better to play relaxing, harmonic music instead of fast tempo rock or beebop jazz. Classical music is particularly good. You can play it outside your head on your stereo, but it is even better if you play it inside, making full use of the capabilities of your imagination.

If you are more comfortable with another form of imagery, you can meditate with that. For example, some people prefer visual imagery. If you are one of those people, you could try a technique that some Buddhist monks use: imagining their meditation teacher floating above their heads, meditating, with the teacher's meditation teacher above his head, and so forth, so that they are visualizing an endless vertical chain of meditation teachers reaching into the sky and beyond.

Another visual technique is to focus on entoptic imagery. That is the name for the lights and sparks and swirls that most people see when they close their eyes. If you don't see them right away, you can create a brighter display by pressing gently on your eyeball through your eyelid. To meditate, all you have to do is watch this imagery with interest, like looking into a kaleidoscope, allowing the shapes and colors to engross you as you wonder what you will see next, or what interesting patterns or pictures will emerge.

If you prefer to be more creative, you can manufacture a scene and then project yourself into it. For example, you could go to a pleasant beach or a secluded mountain cabin or float through the sky on a cloud, either in the daytime or at night under the sparkling stars. The particular scene is unimportant; what matters is that you are comfortable with it and can easily become lost within it.

Many people like to combine types of imagery. For example, you might think the sound of a word while also seeing the word written or printed in any typeface or handwriting you desire. If you visualize yourself at the beach, you could also hear the waves and seagulls, feel the sand supporting your relaxed body, feel the sun warming your skin, and smell the fresh ocean air. In the mountains, you might smell the pines, hear the sparkling brook and woodpeckers in the distance, or feel the warmth of a crackling campfire.

As I've been talking to you, I've noticed that you have been trying out some of these methods already. In fact, you've probably already selected a method that you would like to use for a while. I think it would be a good idea for you to practice a little bit now, so go ahead and use the technique you have chosen for the next several minutes. If you'd like, I can keep talking as you begin, to guide you into a scene. Would you like that? [*If the patient wishes, guide him or her into a pleasant scene, such as the beach or mountains or cloud in the sky, and offer permissive, indirect deepening suggestions and posthypnotic suggestions for continuing the practice, reaching the same level more easily the next time, and improving with practice. For example: "Every time you sit down to meditate and take a nice, deep breath, you will find it easier to go into a deeper and deeper meditative state more and more easily, quickly, and effectively." After a time, stop the patient by continuing the script as follows.]*

Okay, now slowly and gently stop your meditation technique and feel the pleasant glow and maybe even find yourself smiling as you open your eyes. Good. Now, how do you feel? *[Listen to the answer, and affirm and reinforce any pleasant feelings.]* What technique did you select? *[Listen to the answer, and provide any suggestions that will improve the technique.]* Did you encounter any difficulties? *[Resolve any difficulties the patient may have had]* Excellent. You are now a meditator.

Remember now to meditate daily. Schedule time for it. Think of it as "mental hygiene," just like brushing your teeth is dental hygiene. It is a necessary daily practice. Also find a safe, quiet place for your meditation, where you won't be interrupted.

Do your meditating sitting up in a comfortable chair. Eastern yogis meditate sitting on the floor knotted up in a "lotus position," not because there is any magical power in that position, but because they often cannot afford chairs or are unaccustomed to them. We are from a Western civilization and are more accustomed to sitting in chairs, so that is more appropriate for us. Also, if you were to meditate lying down, you might fall asleep and be late for work or an appointment. That is less likely to happen if you are sitting up.

Finally, you will also need to plan a way for timing yourself, at least in the beginning, because most people lose track of time while meditating. Try sitting facing a clock that is easy to read, so that you can see it through a slightly open slit in one eyelid, without having to lift or turn your head. Or place your wristwatch on your lap, or keep its face turned and uncovered so that you can see it easily.

Do you have any questions? *[Answer questions and resolve any difficulties. Continue to reinforce the idea of practicing and of finding it easier and easier to go deeper and deeper each time. Remind the patient that meditation should always be easy and comfortable,*

and that the way to tell if he or she is doing it correctly is whether
or not it is easy and comfortable.]

When the above meditation lesson is completed, the patient will
have experienced some degree of trance. At practically any time
during the lesson, during practice, or during future meditations,
the therapist can begin to add slightly more directive or inten-
tional suggestions, in order to produce specific hypnotic outcomes, to loosen up conscious resistance to surrender, and to
illustrate experientially what "turning it over" (a popular Twelve
Step phrase for surrendering conscious, willful control) means.

The following is an example of how a meditation practice session led naturally into a specific hypnotic intervention:

During a group meditation session that was held every morning in the inpatient chemical dependency treatment program, the therapist leading the session observed one of the
patients wincing in pain. The patient, George, was a 60-year
old man who had been disabled for some time with arthritis
in both knees, and it was obvious that his knees were both-
ering him. As the group continued to meditate, the therapist
walked over to George, leaned down near George's ear, and
suggested in a soft, gentle tone that George become more
deeply relaxed.

He picked up George's hand and slowly released it, noting
that the hand remained floating cataleptically above George's
lap, indicating that George was an excellent hypnotic subject
and was in a deep trance. The therapist asked George to
open his eyes and look at his inflamed knees. He told George,
who had been a pipefitter before he became disabled, that
there were two gas jets, one in each knee, and the flames were
burning hotly and brightly, but that George could lower the
flames by turning the valves, which were located on his
thighs. George then reached down with his other hand and
turned the hallucinated valves, first on one thigh and then
on the other, sighing in relief as he did so. The therapist told

George that the valves would always be there for him, and that he could turn the flames down whenever he needed relief. From that point through the remainder of George's hospitalization, the swelling never recurred and George had markedly improved mobility.

When the other patients expressed amazement at this quick "cure," and began to view the therapist as some sort of magical healer, he deflected this perception by pointing out that George's unconscious mind was very powerful and that George had simply turned his pain over to Higher Power. Perhaps they would be interested in allowing their Higher Power to work for them, too, by helping them recover from chemical dependency.

A PERMISSIVE, INDIRECT APPROACH

Before Erickson came along, most hypnotists employed only direct suggestion and relied heavily on the "prestige" of the "operator." Patients or subjects who would not or could not respond to an imposing, commanding hypnotist were classified as unhypnotizable, and the benefits of clinical hypnosis were unavailable to them. Erickson found ways to make it easy for such people to achieve hypnosis by giving them suggestions in indirect ways and interacting with them in a gentle, permissive manner. By making his suggestions indirectly, he did not sacrifice the ability to lead patients in specific directions. Nor did he, by operating permissively, "water down" his power to influence others. In fact, he used these techniques to dramatically increase the power of hypnosis and therapy.

What is the difference between direct and indirect suggestion, or between a commanding and permissive approach? The difference is largely semantic. Erickson was a master at choosing his words and phrasing his suggestions so that his subjects or patients could feel that they were freely making choices, while, in fact, they were being subtly, unconsciously guided.

The power of Erickson's words and phrases has been of great interest to semanticists, some of whom have analyzed his work from a semantic point of view and written books attempting to explain how he performed his "magic" (Bandler & Grinder, 1975, for instance, whose efforts have given rise to an entire school of therapy, called "Neurolinguistic Programming").

Many different therapeutic techniques fit under the heading "permissive." Of course, almost any technique based on the utilization approach is permissive. In addition, there are therapeutic binds, or offering several alternatives any of which is acceptable; suggestions covering all possibilities of a class of responses; providing a worse alternative; implication; story-telling and metaphor; multilevel or multimeaning communication; and many, many other techniques, some cataloged and described, and others not yet isolated out of Erickson's rich body of work.

Therapeutic binds (Erickson, Rossi, & Rossi, 1976) are semantic devices that offer a patient what seem like free choices, but which actually limit the choices to a narrow range that contains only choices that will be acceptable from the therapeutic point of view. For example, Erickson might inquire whether his patient wanted to enter a light or a deep trance, whether the patient wanted to enter a trance now or later, or whether the patient wanted to go into a trance with eyes open or with eyes closed. Or he might suggest hand levitation by asking which hand will become lighter. Notice that every choice offered involves going into a trance or a hypnotic phenomenon. A chemical dependency therapist might employ this technique by asking a patient if he or she would rather attend an A.A. meeting every day of the week or enter an inpatient treatment program.

A similar technique is to *suggest all possibilities of a class of responses*. To carry the hand levitation induction in the example above further, Erickson might continue to wonder aloud not only which hand would become lighter, but whether one hand or the other would begin to feel heavier while the other hand became lighter, or whether both hands would become lighter, both become heavier, or one or both stay the same, and so forth. In this way, the patient is able to feel that he or she is cooperating with the induction, no matter what happens. In fact, any response at all, including no response, becomes a hypnotic response. Additionally, a long recitation of all the possibilities may begin to overwhelm and confuse the patient, and then the approach verges into a confusion technique. To employ this technique, the chemical dependency therapist might address the same issue as in the example above, but vary it by mentioning that the patient might go to daily A.A. meetings instead of going into an inpatient program, go into an inpatient program instead of going to meetings, go to fewer than seven meetings a week, or stay in denial and do nothing.

Providing a worse alternative is a method Erickson sometimes used when he felt that a patient was inclined to be somewhat, but not completely, resistant. He suggested that the patient take some extreme action, which the patient surely would find distasteful. Yet, even though the patient refused to carry out the precise suggestion, he or she often found a less extreme member of the same class of actions to be quite palatable and would carry out one of these actions "spontaneously." Then, Erickson "settled for" whatever the patient finally came up with. A chemical dependency therapist might employ this technique by demanding that the patient attend 14 A.A. meetings per week, or go into inpatient treatment for six months, and then settle for five or seven meetings per week or one month of inpatient treatment.

Implication is another linguistic device that can be used to compel patients to do specific things, without having to specifically ask for or suggest those things. Erickson was a master at planting meaningful implied suggestions whose importance was initially unrecognized and that had the effect of setting up his patients to later experience unexpected developments.

One method of implied suggestion that Erickson often used was to connect ideas together in ways that implied causality, as when he said things like: "You can go into a trance *as you sit all the way down in that chair*," as if sitting all the way down in the chair somehow caused a trance to occur. Another simple use of implication was the famous one-sentence therapy in which Erickson met a rebellious teenager who had been led to believe that Erickson was going to make him change. As they shook hands, Erickson said impressively: "I don't know *how* you are going to change."

It is easy to make implied suggestions inadvertently. One instance of that occurred when I was working with a nurse who was a very talented demonstration subject. After making two holes painlessly in the back of her hand with a large, sterile needle, she had just successfully demonstrated her ability to keep from bleeding from either hole, and then to bleed from one hole and not the other. I handed her a rather thick wad of tissue to wipe away the blood, whereupon she found herself unable to stop bleeding at all, until I became concerned and gave her a direct suggestion for the bleeding to stop. Only later did we realize that her blood flow had increased in response to the *thick wad* of tissue, which had served as an implied suggestion: Apparently, she unconsciously concluded that a lot of tissue required a lot of blood, and her vascular system responded accordingly.

Alert chemical dependency therapists can find many ways to devise and use implied directives. For example, a therapist might comment: "I wonder how many A.A. meetings you will need to attend before you find a sponsor." Another therapist might mention to a patient how surprised he or she is that the patient has not yet expressed any of the hidden rage, guilt, shame, or fear, etc., and wonders when the patient will do so. Another therapist might tell a patient that, during their next session, the patient is certain to talk about an interesting discovery about himself or herself in relation to addiction, and that the therapist is most curious to find out what it will be.

Storytelling is another technique that Erickson employed often. The stories were often metaphors that contained strong implications about what his patients ought to do to resolve their problems, but which made his points in a manner that was very acceptable to the patients, because they were free to understand and incorporate whatever implications from the stories they wanted or needed to use. Alcoholics Anonymous and other Twelve Step programs are rich with stories, and sending patients to meetings is one sure way of exposing them to stories that are likely to influence them. Once a therapist has been working with chemically dependent patients for a reasonable length of time, the therapist will have seen or heard many interesting and dramatic true stories that can then be told to patients with good effect.

Another indirect hypnotic approach pioneered by Erickson is *multilevel or multimeaning communication* (Erickson & Rossi, 1979). Using this approach, he was able to convey one message to a person's conscious mind, while telling something completely different to the unconscious mind. Dr. Erickson had an acute sense of the multiple meanings of words and phrases, and he knew that his patients' or subjects' responsive unconscious mental processes would consider *all* the meanings of his words, while their conscious processes would *edit out* the meanings that were not appropriate to the immediate context.

Dr. Erickson frequently communicated at multiple levels by loading his communication with minimal cues such as puns or repetitions, or by discussing several different topics that seemed unrelated but had one element in common. An amusing example of this technique was perpetrated on Erickson by his oldest son, Bert, who once engaged in an apparently casual conversation with his father about a number of vacation trips the Erickson family had taken (Erickson, 1967b). As Bert vividly described these vacation memories, Erickson had several urges to offer Bert the car keys. Why? All of the recollections Bert described had one theme in common: They were trips that had been taken in the car. Finally, Erickson realized what Bert was up to and said "No," and Bert laughed and said that at least it had been a good try.

A chemical dependency therapist can begin to communicate in this way by following the scripts presented earlier that describe the process of addiction and recovery, and explain the value of confusion. Generally, merely being attuned to the possibility of communicating at different levels and keeping in mind the multiple meanings of certain words are enough to guide a therapist toward improved use of this kind of communication.

ORDEALS

Often, after securing his patients' trust and promises to cooperate, Erickson prescribed "homework" for them which, they soon discovered, was a benign or therapeutic ordeal. Some ordeals forced patients to face and survive feared experiences, helping them to overcome phobias. One example of this kind of ordeal is the well-known case in which a patient with a fear of eating in public was given the assignment of taking Dr. and Mrs. Erickson out to dinner (Haley, 1973). The evening was filled with a nightmarish series of embarrassments that Erickson had planned in advance with the cooperation of the waitress. After that experience, the patient knew that he could endure almost anything that might happen in an ordinary restaurant.

Another way that Erickson employed ordeals was to link them with symptoms in order to make the symptoms undesirable. One example of this technique is the case of the 65-year-old man who suffered from insomnia and was addicted to sleeping pills (Haley, 1984). The man was getting only two hours of sleep a night. Erickson asked him if he would be willing to give up eight hours of sleep and do some hard work in order to be cured of the insomnia, and the man promised that he would. Knowing that the man hated waxing floors, Erickson told him to stay up all night waxing floors for four consecutive nights, thereby losing only eight hours of sleep (two per night times four). The man lasted just three nights before he decided to lie down and rest before waxing on the fourth night, only to find himself waking up the next morning, having slept the entire night without waxing. In short, the man gave up his insomnia to avoid waxing floors. Note also that this ordeal is also an example of a therapeutic bind: Did the patient prefer insomnia or waxing floors?

An example of an ordeal employed in chemical dependency treatment involved Steve, a tall, thin, 65-year-old man who had been alcoholic most of his adult life and who was also an adult-onset diabetic. He was admitted to the peer group-oriented inpatient alcoholism treatment program at the insistence of his son and daughter-in-law, who had found that, no matter how hard they tried to help him, he had a knack for undermining their every effort.

Steve frustrated the members of his peer group tremendously, because he just couldn't seem to understand what they tried, over and over, to tell him about his alcoholism; or, if he did understand, he didn't seem to care. Their frustration reached a peak when, after they had spent a great deal of time and energy making special arrangements and allowances for him about his diet and other needs related to his diabetes, he was apprehended stealing a candy bar from the hospital store. It was the approach of the treatment program to make the group responsible for the behavior of its members, so an emergency meeting was called to ask the group what it was going to do about Steve's crime.

Their patience was at an end, and they were willing to do almost anything to get through to him. The therapist decided to take advantage of this willingness to create an ordeal that might break through his delusional system. He proposed to the group that, since Steve was likely to die unless he admitted the reality of his alcoholism, they should take him out on a pass to shop for coffins. Perhaps the reality of looking at real coffins in a real mortuary would shock him into being able to see the truth of his situation.

The group was sufficiently frustrated to agree to the plan, and also to the addition of one more stipulation: that Steve's assignment would be to find out whether he would need an extra long coffin (because of his height), or if he would be able to make do with a a coffin of average length by having his legs broken to make him fit. Steve joked and laughed throughout the pass-planning process, as if he were daring the group to try to change him while inviting them to fail. This attitude added to the group's frustration and increased its willingness to carry out the plan.

Steve and a handful of other patients located a mortuary and visited it the following day. The day after that, they read a report to the full group describing what had happened and how they felt about it. Those who accompanied Steve felt frustrated, frightened, and appalled, and Steve felt "happy." He had walked through the experience without being the least bit affected: He sauntered into the mortuary, engaged the proprietor in small talk, conveniently neglected to carry out his assignment (to ask whether he would need a long coffin or a standard one), and behaved throughout that day and the next in his usual, happy-go-lucky, unconcerned manner.

Although Steve was unaffected, the rest of the group was in an uproar. They simply couldn't believe that anyone could be so completely shut off from reality. The therapist explained carefully and at length that Steve's inability to grasp the seriousness of his condition was a symptom of alcoholism, that they, too, had the disease, and that they, too, were no doubt well defended in areas of which they were unaware. Then, with Steve looking on from the sidelines, the group began to explore the ways in which other patients were blind to the reality of their own conditions, and the discussion led to several important breakthroughs. The ordeal had failed in its original goal of breaking through Steve's wall of defenses, but it had accomplished another, perhaps more valuable, one of showing the other 25 patients the reality of their disease.

4

The Group as Patient: Facilitating a Healthy Group Process in an Unhealthy Group

WHY GROUPS?

Groups are by far the most widely used modality in chemical dependency treatment. The preference for groups may have evolved because of the fact that most chemical dependency professionals have strong ties with Alcoholics Anonymous, and A.A. is primarily group-oriented. The strong bonding among members that takes place in A.A. meetings is one of the most powerful attractors of new members to the program, and those who conduct counseling and therapy groups have learned to take advantage of the same inherent magnetism that arises when alcoholics and addicts get together and honestly share their pains, hopes, and successes.

Another reason for using a group approach is the fact that many individual therapists, when they find themselves face to face with a chemically dependent patient, soon discover that they are *outnumbered*. This statement is less facetious than it would seem to be on the surface. Individual therapists really are out-numbered, since they face both an addicted patient *and* his or her disease, which tips the balance of power to two-to-one against the therapist. An addicted patient alone can often prove too much for all but the most skilled and experienced individual therapists, since addicted people can be so adept at hiding their addiction or at complying convincingly while inwardly resisting. When these "skills" are combined with the malignant power of the disease (which behaves exactly as it would if it actually pos-sessed its victims or dwelled independently within them), the odds of successful treatment often approach zero. Therapists who avoid the traps inherent in individual therapy by dealing primarily with groups of addicts find that the odds often improve greatly. Instead of battling addiction in a game that addicts have mastered (dealing with individual challenges and criticisms), a therapist who is well versed in group dynamics can much more easily outmaneuver addiction by forcing it to play the therapist's game on the therapist's turf.

Mistrust is a major difficulty in psychotherapy with patients who have had repeated addiction-related run-ins with authority. They tend to perceive a therapist as just another authority figure, and then tune him or her out in the same way that they have tuned out so many well-intentioned but often misguided spouses, employers, police officers, judges, preachers, and doctors. This mistrust occurs in both individual and group settings, and, if it is not handled appropriately, it invariably interferes with effective therapeutic communication.

Even therapists or counselors who are recovering alcoholics and addicts encounter this authority figure syndrome. Jaded and cyn-ical patients often see recovering treatment staff as turncoats and sellouts, instead of accepting them as people who truly under-stand. Besides, a therapist who once practiced an addiction has only one life story to tell, and that story may not be relevant to a broad range of patients. Any given patient is much more likely to hear a story he or she can relate to among a group of peers, or, even better, at an A.A. meeting, where a wide variety of people, from diverse walks of life, can be counted on to talk about many different types and degrees of experiences of addiction and recovery.

Chemically dependent people deeply long for and treasure the opportunity to be members of a bonded group—to be accepted and to belong. Although they often appear on the surface to be confident, self-contained, and independent, they very often harbor deep and painful feelings of shame, self-loathing, and, above all, loneliness. People who hate themselves cannot readily accept love from other people, especially from professionals whom they deem at some level to be "better" than they are. It is difficult, however, to discount or deny the love of one drunk or addict for another. The ready believability and acceptability of love from peers is what makes a peer group so powerful. Groups and membership in them are very strong reinforcers and influencers of the behavior of group members. The power generated in peer groups of addicts goes way beyond the strength of influence found in what most people think of as peer pressure. It is more like "peer pressure squared."

A therapist can expect to be much more effective with many more addicted patients by harnessing the power of "peer pressure squared" than by struggling against high odds to make individuals change one at a time. A therapist can gain this kind of power by accepting the fact that he or she *is* an authority figure and not a typical group member. From this stance, the therapist can deal with the group as an entity and bypass resistance by communicating with individual patients *through* the group instead of directly.

Two additional distinct advantages arise from the use of a group approach, and both are more concerned with the health and enjoyment of the therapist than of the patients (although it is difficult to say who is benefiting more, since healthy, happy therapists are more likely than harried, angst-ridden ones to deliver quality services). The first of these advantages is the fact that therapists don't have to work as hard in the long run if their groups have a strong and healthy group process. The second is the wealth of opportunities for creative expression and interesting challenges that working with groups offers.

Therapists who rely on a healthy group process are freed from having to worry about what each patient is going to get out of each group session, and from having to do all or most of the work. Instead of constantly dwelling on details and trying to "therapize" every patient, the therapist does most of the work in the beginning, setting up a healthy process. Once this task is done, the therapist can lean back and watch the therapy happen, needing only to intervene occasionally in order to keep the group process headed in a constructive direction. Besides, if a therapist is working harder at a patient's recovery than the patient is, something is wrong. Either the patient is successfully resisting treatment or the therapist is erring in the codependent direction (or both).

A final advantage of group therapy is that it can be extremely interesting. If individual therapy is like playing a solo instrument (say, a clarinet), then group therapy is like playing on a huge pipe organ or conducting an orchestra. Groups are more challenging, complex, and multileveled. One patient's dynamics can be extremely fascinating, but that degree of interest multiplied by the number of patients in a group, plus the complex dynamics of the group itself, yields up a feast capable of satisfying almost any stimulus hunger. Therapists who crave learning, growth, and opportunities for creative expression are much more likely to thrive doing group therapy than they are working exclusively with individuals.

BASIC ASSUMPTIONS ABOUT GROUPS

The group therapy techniques described in this chapter are based on one core assumption: that a group is an *individual entity,* and that this entity has its own dynamics that are quite distinct from, and operate at a different level from, the dynamics of the individuals who make up the group.

A group is an entity made up of people, just as a human being is an entity made up of organs, and organs are entities made up of cells. A group is more than just a loose collection of individual personalities. It has its own motives, drives, and behavior tendencies—its own "personality." And, just as an individual personality can be influenced by therapy, so too can the group's personality.

When a person's personality decides to get up and walk across a room, all of that person's organs and cells cross the room too, and many of the organs and cells join together in a cooperative, interactive way to carry out the personality's decision. The organs and cells join in this complex, cooperative behavior even though they do not know the personality's reasons for deciding to cross the room, or that their behavior contributed to the person's crossing the room. They cooperate to carry out the decision automatically, and they are not aware of the meaning of the behavior from the point of view of the personality which instigated the behavior.

Groups of people function in much the same way. Individual members cooperate in complex, interactive ways to carry out group decisions and actions, even though they do not understand what the actions mean from the point of view of the group, or even that their behavior *serves* the group at all. They understand their behavior primarily, and often exclusively, from their individual points of view alone. In a sense, their behavior is "controlled" by the group; they take orders from the group; but they are usually unaware of either the control or the orders.

Therapists who communicate with and influence groups, at the level of group process or the group "entity," can influence group members in very powerful ways by orchestrating group behaviors which require that individual members behave in desired ways in order to accomplish the group behavior that is being orchestrated. When individual members carry out these desired behaviors, they often have no idea why they are doing so, and they are generally not in a position to resist. In other words, therapists proficient in influencing groups can influence individuals by "going through" the groups of which the individuals are members in order to do it.

The ability to communicate with and influence group process is a very powerful tool whose power has been demonstrated countless times throughout history, in both positive and negative ways. Practically all successful politicians, entertainers, religious figures, and cult leaders owe a good part of their success to their ability to influence groups. Some of the obvious or acknowledged masters at influencing group process are Mahatma Gandhi, Billy Graham, Clarence Darrow, Frank Sinatra, the Beatles, Adolph Hitler, Jim Jones, and Charles Manson.

Milton Erickson's work provides valuable inspiration for anyone interested in developing such techniques. Many powerful methods can be created by taking some of his techniques for influencing the behavior of individuals and applying them to groups. This chapter contains descriptions of some techniques that were devised in this way, including: developing response-attentiveness (Erickson & Rossi, 1979); establishing principles to guide future decision-making; backward communication (Lovern, 1980); sacrifices (Lovern, 1980; Cutter, 1975); utilization (Erickson, 1967a); offering several alternatives, any of which is acceptable (Haley, 1973); encouraging or predicting resistance (Haley, 1973); providing a worse alternative (Haley, 1973); confusion-restructuring (Erickson, Rossi, & Rossi, 1976); shock, surprise, and humor (Erickson & Rossi, 1979); and arousing one emotion and switching to another.

GOALS AND TECHNIQUES OF GROUP THERAPY

Group methods presented in this chapter were created with two kinds of goals in mind: *outcome goals*, or desired behavioral outcomes for the patients; and *process goals*, or goals related to the functioning of the groups (Lovern & Zohn, 1982).

Outcome goals were (a) to create surrender experiences in individual patients; (b) to help patients to perceive clearly, and begin working to overcome, their addiction-related physical, cognitive, emotional, interpersonal, and other problems; and (c) basically to function as a sort of Alcoholics Anonymous boot camp, so that patients would be able to easily, smoothly, and knowledgeably enter and participate in A.A. and other relevant Twelve-Step programs.

Process goals were related to whether groups would function as positive, recovery-supporting systems, or as unhealthy, sabotaging conspiracies. Groups needed to be systems which (a) consistently made decisions that supported the recoveries of members; (b) cared lovingly about members, but not in a way that shielded them from the discomfort that was necessary for recovery; and (c) could always be guided or directed by therapists, to ensure that the above two conditions could be maintained, and that denial, avoidance, and other symptoms of addiction would not erupt and undermine treatment.

INDIRECT HYPNOTIC COMMUNICATION WITH GROUPS

This section contains descriptions and examples of a number of group therapy techniques that were created by modifying some of Erickson's individual therapy techniques for use in groups.

DEVELOPING RESPONSE-ATTENTIVENESS

Erickson and Rossi (1979) defined response-attentiveness as "a state of extreme attentiveness in responding to the nuances of communication presented by the therapist." In other words, this state is one of openness and receptivity to hypnotic suggestions.

A good example of response-attentiveness is found in a story told by a young psychologist of his first encounter with Erickson (personal communication). The psychologist had driven many hours to the Erickson home in Phoenix and was tired and anxious about meeting his "idol." As the door opened, he saw that Erickson, sitting in his wheelchair, had answered the door himself. His confusion and apprehension mounted as he stood in the doorway, not knowing what to do or say next. Erickson saw the psychologist's confusion and realized that it had caused his response-attentiveness to heighten, so he decided to use the heightened response-attentiveness to play a humorous prank. Erickson looked up and gazed deeply into the psychologist's eyes, then lowered his chin to his chest in a series of short movements, closing his eyes as he did so. As Erickson's head lowered, the psychologist found his own head lowering too, and he entered a deep hypnotic trance. His response-attentiveness attuned him to Erickson's nuances of communication, so that he responded quickly to the nonverbal suggestion to lower his head and go into a trance.

With a group, response-attentiveness is a collective phenomenon in which the therapist is the object of intensely focused attention by all group members and by the group itself, and can therefore exert considerable influence over group behavior. Without response-attentiveness, it is impossible to use any of the other techniques that follow. What is the use of communicating in sophisticated, multilevel, subtly directive ways if the audience is paying attention to something or someone else?

Many speakers, teachers, or leaders can get attention and sometimes arouse response-attentiveness in their audiences simply by asking for it, by pounding a gavel, or by similar ceremonial behavior. Given the dynamics of groups of alcoholics and addicts, just asking is usually not enough. Addicts' defensiveness, compliance, people-pleasing, and intellectuality allow only superficial attention. Greater openness is required and it can be elicited by a number of different methods.

One method is for the therapist to enter the therapy room in an attention- and curiosity-arousing manner.

The therapist waited for the group to gather and seat itself, then waited a bit longer for the group to become impatient for him to arrive (but not later than the precise group starting time). Finally, he strode brusquely into the room, carrying a clipboard and wearing an intense facial expression which conveyed an emotion that lay somewhere between anger and determination. After seating himself, he glared as his eyes slowly scanned the room. Then, he raised an eyebrow, shifted to an introspective expression, and began to flip through sheets on his clipboard. As he pointed at one item on a particular sheet, he smiled broadly and nodded his head knowingly, implying that the sheet contained information that he was about to find very useful. Then, he looked up, seeming to be surprised that all eyes were on him, expectantly waiting for direction from him. He paused for a few seconds and the level of tension rose, until he sat erect and looked attentive, indicating that it was time to begin. From that point on, the group was finely attuned to the therapist's behavior, which allowed the therapist to have a profound influence on the proceedings by making small gestures, changes of voice inflection, or subtly worded statements.

Because of a good job of acting, incorporating expressions and gestures that aroused curiosity, along with suitable props (the clipboard and a pen), the therapist captured the attention of the group. Drama and props can be very useful in establishing response-attentiveness in a group, as the next example illustrates:

The therapist entered the therapy room on Monday morning, carrying a cardboard box that measured about 1 foot by 1 foot by 1 foot. With a broad, sweeping gesture, he placed the box on the floor in front of him. Throughout the group session, he repeatedly adjusted its location, patted it, and placed his feet on top of it. At the end of the session, he picked it up and left. At no time did he comment on the box, open it, or let anyone know what it was for or what was in it.

On Tuesday, he again brought the box. He behaved in a similar manner and again left with the box, which remained unexplained. On Wednesday, he had the box again. When patients asked about the box, he answered evasively, saying that the box contained "something very important" or pointing out that the group had important items of business to attend to, and that knowing what was in the box was not one of them. Thursday came around, and the therapist had the box again. By this day, all eyes were riveted to the box and to the therapist, who acted coolly as if the box and its contents were of no particular consequence. Nevertheless, during pauses he gently touched or slightly repositioned the box. Again, he took the box away at the end of the session.

On Friday, the box appeared once again and it was too much for the group to stand. Nearly begging, members of the group asked what was in the box. Finally seeming to make a small concession, the therapist asked what the group was willing to do to have what was in the box. When it was clear that the group was willing to pass a rule he had been trying to get them to pass for a long time, he relented. After the rule was passed, with the provision that once it was passed, it could not be rescinded, he presented the group with the contents of the box.

After slowly and dramatically opening the box, the therapist pulled out an old, broken sports trophy which he had purchased at a thrift shop. The name of the sport depicted on the trophy was a homonym for the last name of one of the patients, who happened to be in nearly unshakable denial at that point in his treatment. The nameplate on the trophy was covered with strips that said: "THE HARRY X. MEMORIAL MOST HOPELESS TROPHY" (with X being the first initial of both Harry's last name and the sport depicted in the trophy). The therapist presented the trophy to the group without explanation, saying that he hoped the group could find some use for it.

During the entire week that the therapist brought the box, all members of the group were desperate to know what was in it, causing the group's and its members' awareness of even the most subtle communicative behaviors by the therapist to be heightened. When the trophy finally emerged from the box, Harry got the message about his denial, the therapist got his rule passed, and the group felt skunked again, realizing that "You *can* con a con," and that their alcoholism had once again gotten them into an undesirable situation. Meanwhile, the group maintained a wary alertness about the therapist so as not to be "tricked" again. As a consequence, its response-attentiveness remained high.

Countless other examples may be given of methods that enhance the response-attentiveness of groups, but effective approaches usually contain several key steps: First, a therapist should capture the group's attention immediately, by doing something dramatic, humorous, anxiety-provoking, or shocking. Then, the therapist should pose a dilemma or puzzle, or in some way arouse curiosity or create a need in the group for information that only the therapist can provide. Finally, the therapist should establish with the group that the only way to get that information is to pay close attention to and/or think hard about subtle behaviors produced by the therapist. Paying close attention to and thinking hard about what the therapist is doing constitute response-attentiveness.

ESTABLISHING PRINCIPLES TO GUIDE FUTURE DECISION-MAKING

A therapist can guide the long-term behavior of a group by getting it to establish key principles which will have consequences that the group cannot at the moment foresee. The best principles to establish are meta-decisions—that is, rules about how to make future decisions—which have universal appeal or with which the group cannot disagree. Once a group has established a principle (or set of principles) for guiding its decisions, the therapist can keep the group perpetually on a desired course by reminding it of the principle (or principles) each time it considers a decision.

For example, suppose a group follows a therapist's suggestion and officially adopts the principle that it will base all future decisions on whether the decisions *contribute to or advance recovery from addiction*. Later, when the group is considering whether to allow its members certain privileges, overlook or punish some behavior of a member, or elect a particular member to a position of leadership (or make any routine decision), the therapist can ask the group how the decision it is considering will contribute to recovery.

If the group is considering rewarding some of its members with weekend passes even though those members have not been working on their recovery for example, the therapist can point out that none of the members being considered for passes completed their written homework that week or were represented by family members at the last family therapy session. If the group is basing its decisions on whether they will advance recovery, it should consider making the privileges or passes conditional on these factors—"Or is this group just interested in doling out 'perks?'" Of course, an intelligent member may raise the issue that passes themselves can be therapeutic. The therapist can respond by agreeing that passes can be therapeutic, "but here is an opportunity to advance recovery *beyond* what the pass alone can do. Does this group want to seize that opportunity and get all the recovery it can, or is it willing to settle for less and *give up* on trying to help its members with their family and other problems? Is that how you drank or used? When you had an opportunity to get high, did you go for it, or did you say 'Nah, it's too much trouble'?" If the group offers additional resistance, the therapist can point out examples of how failure to do homework or involve family members in treatment has contributed to relapse in recently discharged members.

If a member behaves irresponsibly by failing to follow through on a commitment (clearly an "alcoholic behavior"), and the group tries to overlook it, the therapist can point out that the behavior is a core symptom of addiction and, since the group decided that its actions must support recovery, it cannot ignore the behavior.

If the group then begins to lecture that member (the typical response), the therapist can raise the issue of whether lecturing will advance recovery: "How many times have you been 'chewed out' or 'called on the carpet' by a boss or some other authority figure, and did it ever get you to stop drinking or using? Besides, it's easy to lecture somebody, but lecturing is a poor substitute for action. What is the group going to *do* about this member's irresponsible behavior?" Typically, groups then suggest punishment. The therapist can respond by asking the group if punishment ever helped any of them to stop drinking or using, "or did it just fill you with resentment and make you want to drink or use 'at' the people who punished you?" At this point, the therapist can suggest a sacrifice, in which the entire group gives up or offers to give up something of value in order to show the group's love for the offending member and to use the member's guilt against his or her addiction.

If a group is considering electing its most capable member to be their leader, the therapist can point out that the group is missing a valuable opportunity to advance recovery, since the most capable member will not grow from being the leader: "The group is just trying to find an 'easier, softer way' to get its work done." The therapist can reason that if the group instead selects a member who needs to learn how to lead, how to plan, or how to interact assertively with others, then that person's recovery will be advanced, while the other members' recoveries will also be advanced by having to learn patience as a result of having such a member as their leader. This line of reasoning led to a series of group leaders who were cognitively impaired, shy, and interpersonally inept. While this selection did effectively advance recovery in the way described, it also had the advantage of making it easier for the therapist to influence group decisions.

A final example of establishing a principle to guide future group behavior is one that relies on a preliminary lecture or "pep-talk" given by the therapist at the beginning of a group therapy session. In this case, the therapist wants to make sure that the group listens and responds in the most helpful manner to a patient's Discharge Plan (a written plan outlining the patient's problems, proposed solutions, and therapy and A.A. schedule):

> We're going to hear Joe Smith's Discharge Plan today, but, before we do, I want to make sure that the group understands how to listen when he reads it, and what kind of comments to make after he's done.
>
> A Discharge Plan is probably the most important thing that any of you will do in this program. It's your list of the problems you'll be facing, including as many of the dangers to your sobriety as you and the group can think of, and what you intend to do about each one. In other words, it's your *survival vehicle*. It's the only thing you'll have to take with you when you leave, to help you stay alive. So it had better be good!
>
> Your Discharge Plan is like your rowboat for getting off this island. If the boat's in good shape, if you have both oars, and if you're in good enough physical condition to row all the way to shore, then you might have a chance to make it. But there are lots of dangers out there. You might have to row against a strong current, or there might be a storm, or a shark might attack. You have to be ready for anything that might happen. You can't just set out casually without a plan. You need to know what the weather forecast is, where the strong currents are, and whether the waters you plan to row through have sharks or sea monsters.
>
> It's interesting to compare the chances of getting out of here alive to the chances of surviving a trip to the moon. Lots of astronauts have survived their trips to the moon and back—except for a few who died on the launch pad before they even took off. The chances of making it to the moon and back alive were pretty good, weren't they? Well, they were a heck of a lot better than the chances of surviving when you leave here.
>
> If we do a really good job of treating you for your addic-

tion, the very best chance you have of staying clean and sober for just a year after you leave here is fifty-fifty. Do you know what that means? That means that you're a lot more likely to survive a trip to the moon than you are to survive a trip out of here. Think of it. A trip all the way to the moon and back is safer than being discharged.

Why is a trip to the moon so safe? Because it's so well planned. They have hundreds of people working full-time on every phase of those trips. Engineers take years to design and test the moon rockets, and they perform thousands of calculations and check them again and again to make sure they're right. Finally, just before the moon rocket takes off, they inspect everything on it.

Now, suppose the inspectors find a problem in the life support system. Imagine what would happen if they said to themselves: "It's just a little air leak. It's not too bad. Nobody will notice." Or, what if they thought: "Those astronauts want to go to the moon real bad, but if I tell someone about this leak, the mission might be canceled. I really like those astronauts, and I don't want to upset them, so I won't say anything." That would be crazy, wouldn't it? They could kill the astronauts.

If they want the astronauts to survive all the way to the moon and back, the inspectors have to look hard for problems. I mean, they have to dig. And they have to report every little problem, even every suspected problem.

Well, that's what you need to do when Joe Smith reads his Discharge Plan. You need to recognize that whether or not he has a good plan can make the difference between whether he lives or dies.

If you think you see a problem, should you tell yourself: "That's not so bad; it won't make any difference"? [*The group says "No."*] Should you think: "I like Joe, and I don't want to make him mad, so I won't say anything."? [*The group says "No."*] That's right. You should run this thing through a fine tooth comb, and point out any problem that even just might be there. And then maybe Joe will have a good chance to make it.

Now, let's hear Joe's Discharge Plan.

If therapists do not begin their groups with this kind of introduction at least some of the time, they run the risk of overseeing a sickness-supporting, nudge-and-wink kind of group process that invariably falls back to the path of least resistance. If they do clarify for members how they are to behave, and offer a convincing and motivating rationale for that kind of behavior, their groups will be consistently effective and rewarding.

BACKWARD COMMUNICATION

Backward communication is actually a form of the Socratic method. Benjamin Franklin, in his autobiography (Franklin, 1968), described the usefulness he found in the Socratic method as a tool for influencing others:

> While I was intent on improving my language, I met with an English grammar . . . having at the end of it two little sketches on the arts of rhetoric and logic, the latter finishing with a dispute in the Socratic method; and soon after I procured Xenophon's *Memorable Things of Socrates*, wherein there are many examples of the same method. I was charmed with it, adopted it, dropped my abrupt contradiction and positive argumentation, and put on the humble inquirer; . . . I found this method the safest for myself and very embarrassing to those against whom I used it; therefore, I took delight in it, practiced it continually, and grew very artful and expert in drawing people, even of superior knowledge, into concessions, the consequences of which they did not foresee, entangling them in difficulties out of which they could not extricate themselves, and so obtaining victories that neither myself nor my cause always deserved. (pp. 29–30)

Backward communication was developed with this rationale: If a therapist tells a patient that the patient is addicted (or communicates some related idea or interpretation), and the patient denies it, then the intervention is a failure and the patient's denial is even stronger than it would have been if no intervention had been attempted. If, on the other hand, the therapist manages somehow to get the *patient* to try to communicate the same idea *to the therapist*, as if it were the patient's idea, then the therapist can simply accept it. In the second case, the interaction ends with agreement and cooperation, instead of with frustration and hardened resistance. The technique that achieves this result is called backward communication, because the ideas the therapist wants the patient to receive are directed backward from the patient to the therapist.

Backward communication can be used with groups as well as with individuals. In essence, it consists of leading the group, by a series of questions, to a conclusion or decision chosen in advance by the therapist. In one variation of this technique, the therapist leads the group in a process that inevitably causes one or more patients to confess that they have engaged in a certain behavior symptomatic of addiction, or similar behaviors. The therapist is able to avoid stirring up the resistance and denial that would normally arise from accusing patients of having the symptom by instead simply listening to and believing the confessions, thus completing the backward communication.

To elicit these confessions, the therapist follows a standard format: After selecting a target behavior, he or she (a) reminds the group of an established principle (relying on a decision put in place by the technique described above); (b) asks the group to describe examples of ways in which a member of the group might abuse or avoid following the principle; and (c) after hearing the group's initial global and general cases, asks for progressively more specific examples, until the descriptions more and more closely approximate the target behavior. At this point, members who have engaged in behaviors similar to the behavior toward which the questioning seems to be leading begin to confess in order to avoid the relatively more undesirable prospect of waiting until the group names them as violators.

To successfully carry out this technique, the therapist needs to construct a hierarchy of behaviors, with the target behavior at its center. The first step is to choose the target behavior. A target behavior is some specific behavioral symptom of addiction that a patient is known to have recently engaged in, for example, sneaking a visit with a lover outside of visiting hours. The next step is to figure out to what more general category of behaviors that specific behavior belongs, and then to what more general category that behavior belongs, etc., until the therapist arrives at a very general behavior. In visual terms, the target behavior represents the bullseye of a target, with the progressively more general categories forming the concentric outer rings.

In this case, George sneaking a visit with his girlfriend Mary is the target behavior (or the bullseye). This specific behavior is an example of the more general behavior of addicts sneaking visits with lovers or spouses (the next larger concentric ring). This behavior is an example of placing a visit with a lover or spouse ahead of one's own recovery (the next larger ring). This behavior is an example of the even more general behavior of making anything more important than recovery (the next larger ring). This behavior is an example of the still more general behavior of lying or pretending about one's motivation for recovery. And this behavior is an example of the global behavior of "ripping off" or cheating a treatment program (the outermost ring).

The following is an example of how a therapist might carry out a backward communication strategy to elicit a confession from George about his unauthorized visit with Mary, and to make clear that the unauthorized visit was not just a rule violation, but a symptom of addiction and, therefore, an incident of life-or-death significance. The basic process calls for the therapist to begin at the outermost ring of the target and work inexorably inward, toward the bullseye:

The therapist began by asking the group: "What are we here for?" When the group did not answer immediately, the therapist asked Bob, a fairly new patient: "Bob, what are *you* here for?"

Bob said: "To get sober."

The therapist replied: "To get sober. Do you mean just to quit drinking? Or do you have something else in mind?"

Bob answered: "To quit drinking."

The therapist then queried another patient, one who had been in the program somewhat longer: "Mike, is that all we're here for, just to quit drinking?"

Mike stated: "No. I know I have to quit drinking, but it's not that simple. I have to work a program."

The therapist reinforced Mike, saying: "That's right. You have to work a program. Anybody can quit drinking. Most of you here have quit drinking hundreds of times. Am I right?" A number of patients agreed, some laughing. "You need to do more. You need to work a program, as Mike says, so that you don't start drinking again. How important is it to work a program, Steve?" the therapist asked an advanced patient.

"It's very important," said Steve.

"I mean, how important is it compared to other things?" asked the therapist.

Steve proclaimed: "It has to come first."

"It has to come first, before anything else?" the therapist continued.

"Before *anything* else," Steve affirmed.

The therapist said "Good, I agree with you on that," then changed direction. "Well, if it's true that you have to put your recovery first, how might an alcoholic or addict rip off a program? How about you, Dan? I'm sure that *you* can think of ways to rip off a program, can't you?" Here, the therapist was referring indirectly to a recent incident in which Dan had behaved dishonestly and was characterized as ripping off the program. "What's one way you can think of that an alcoholic or addict might rip off a treatment program?"

"Drinking while you're in treatment," Dan declared.

"That's true, Dan. Drinking while you're in treatment is definitely one way to rip off a program. And that would be a slip. Now, you all know that a slip doesn't begin with the first drink. Something always comes before the first drink, like a thought: the thought of having that drink. And what comes before that thought? Other thoughts and other behaviors do. In fact, a lot of things happen that lead up to the first drink. If you're going to wait until someone drinks in treatment to do something about the slip that's coming, you'll be too late. If you really want to help an alcoholic or addict, you have to look for more subtle things. What's a more subtle way to rip off a program, Ernie?"

Ernie looked puzzled for a moment, then said: "Lying."

"Lying in what way, Ernie?" inquired the therapist.

"You know, like pretending. Saying you believe in something you don't."

"Oh, I see," the therapist commented. "Acting like you believe in something, not because you do, but so that other people will be impressed and give you something you want. Right?"

"Yeah, something like that," Ernie affirmed.

"I like that," praised the therapist. "It's dishonest and it's subtle. Fred, can you think of an example of what Ernie's talking about? An example of pretending to believe in something when you don't, so that you can work some kind of angle?"

Fred, being somewhat new to the unit, and still full of denial and resistance, said: "Yeah, I can think of doing something I don't believe in: Sitting in these damn groups and putting up with your B.S., and then having to go to those stupid A.A. meetings, when all I want to do is quit drinking."

"Well, now, if that isn't just about the sickest thinking I've heard in a long time," the therapist observed, talking about rather than directly to Fred. "I hope the group will help this sick man understand that there's more to getting well than

just quitting drinking. Alcoholism is a disease. If you want
to get well from the disease, you have to put up with the
treatment. A.A. and these groups *are* the treatment for his
disease. Trying to recover from alcoholism without going
along with the treatment is like going to the hospital com-
plaining of a ruptured appendix and refusing to let the doctor operate.

"Can somebody else think of a way that an alcoholic or
addict might lie and pretend to believe in something, as a
manipulation?" The therapist looked at the group, obviously
waiting for members to raise their hands. None did. "Well,
what an eager group," he said sarcastically. "I can see how
willing you all are to work hard on your recovery in this meeting. Boy, those hands just shot up." Then, the therapist
waited, frowning. Gradually, although looking somewhat
offended, several members began to raise their hands. One
of those was Paul. "How about you, Paul?"

Paul said: "O.K., I have an example. How about pretending you want to get clean and sober, when you really
don't want to?"

"That's great, Paul. You really do think like an addict," the
therapist commented. "Pretending you want to get clean and
sober," he repeated, savoring the words. Then, the therapist
repeated the second half of Paul's sentence: "When you really
don't want to—you mean, an alcoholic or addict might not
want to get clean and sober? He might actually put something ahead of recovery?"

"That's right," agreed Paul.

"Well, gee, what kinds of things might an addict put ahead
of his recovery?" the therapist wondered. "Do *you* have any
idea . . ." the therapist asked, while looking directly at Bob.
But before Bob could answer, the therapist wheeled his head
around to face the other side of the room and fixed his eyes
on Frank; then, with a slightly raised eyebrow, he continued:
". . . Frank?"

Frank, thinking the therapist had wanted Bob to answer

the question, was startled at first when he realized that it was
he who was being asked, then regained his composure and
answered: "His job."

"Yes, I've seen addicts put their job ahead of their recovery," the therapist confirmed. "What else might an addict put
ahead of recovery?"

"Staying out of jail," said Frank.

Slowly nodding, the therapist said: "I agree. I can imagine
an addict wanting to stay out of jail more than he wants to
recover. But what do you suppose he'd do once he got off?"

"Probably go get loaded," Frank predicted.

"That sounds reasonable, Frank," the therapist agreed.
Now, how about you, Jim. What's something else an addict
might put ahead of recovery?"

"I don't know," replied Jim.

"You don't know?" the therapist repeated in an astonished
tone. "Come on. You've been out there drinking and using
and conning and shooting angles for twenty years, and you
don't know what an addict might put ahead of his recovery?
You've got to be kidding."

"O.K.," said Jim. "How about getting laid?"

The therapist looked pleased. "Ah, yes. getting laid.
Keeping a supply of love available. So, you think an addict
might put his love supply ahead of his recovery. Is that right,
Jim?"

"That's right," Jim acknowledged.

"So how might an addict do that?" the therapist asked the
group. "How might an addict put his love supply ahead of
his recovery?"

Phil suggested: "He might want to spend more time with
his lover than he spends on his recovery."

"You mean, he might prefer to spend more evenings with
her than he spends at A.A. meetings?"

"Yeah," said Phil. "He might even tell people that he's
going to an A.A. meeting, and then wind up at her place."

"So that he could be 'wined and dined,'" observed the

therapist, with a leer. "Have any of you ever preferred to be 'wined and dined' by a hot little number instead of working on your recovery?" This question evoked a chorus of yeses from the group. The therapist commented: "I thought some of you might have had some experience along those lines.

"So, that's how an addict might put his love interest ahead of his recovery. But how about *in here*? How might an addict put his love interest ahead of his recovery in this program? Wait a minute. Before we talk about that, let me ask the group what effect it would have on the addict to put his love interest ahead of his recovery in this program. Mark, what do you think?"

Mark ventured his opinion that "He probably wouldn't get anything out of being here."

The therapist inquired, "Do you think he'd be wasting his time?"

"Yeah, he would be wasting his time."

"And would he be wasting the group's time? And my time? And the government's money?"

Mark looked thoughtful. "Yes, I guess he would."

Then, raising his voice gradually as he spoke, to a decidedly angry pitch, the therapist went on: "So, he'd be here under false pretenses, *lying* to you and to the staff, *wasting* a bed in this program that's needed by some addict or alcoholic who really wants to recover. That would be the same as *killing* a sick addict, wouldn't it? And he'd be *stealing*, too, stealing the money that's paying for him to stay here—and that amounts to thousands and thousands of dollars—while he uses us to help him launch his little 'nookie' plans.

"What would you guys think of somebody like that? Would you like him? Would you trust him? Would you want him in your group?"

Tom piped up: "I wouldn't want him around. If all he wants is to get laid, he oughta get out and go do it."

"Anybody else have similar feelings?" the therapist asked, and a number of other patients voiced similar sentiments.

Then, the therapist added another variable: "What effect would a guy like that have on the group? That's an important question, because the group is your treatment, your support. What effect would somebody like that being in the group have on the quality of your treatment?"

Tom spoke again: "He'd water it down."

Steve added: "Yeah, he might bring us all down with him."

"Well," the therapist observed, "since a guy like that is so undesirable, the group ought to do everything it can to spot him and weed him out. How would he act? How might an addict put his love interest ahead of his recovery in this program? Bob?"

Bob guessed, "He'd probably be thinking about her all the time."

"That's true," agreed the therapist. "He probably would be. But how would he *act*?"

"Bob pondered briefly, then said: "Maybe he'd make a lot of phone calls."

"Who would he be calling, Bob?" the therapist inquired.

"Oh, maybe his girlfriend or his wife," Bob answered.

Just then, Al burst in: "All right, all right! It's me you're talking about isn't it? I've been making phone calls to my wife outside of phone hours. But I'm not trying to get laid. I just want to know how my kids are doing."

"It sounds like Al has a guilty conscience, group," commented the therapist. "He *says* he just wants to know how his kids are. I suppose we should believe him, shouldn't we, since he's been so honest up to now," the therapist observed sarcastically. "Well, even if he's telling the truth, the fact remains that he's still been putting something ahead of his recovery. So the group needs to do something to help him get honest.

"Are there any others who've been sneaking phone calls? Why not get honest and 'fess up? You know it'll come out eventually. And besides, you're really only cheating yourself by putting those phone calls ahead of your recovery. Or maybe, if you don't have the *balls* to admit it yourself, maybe somebody else who knows about it will call you on it." There followed a long pause, with the therapist looking searchingly at every patient.

"Well," the therapist finally broke the silence. "Maybe nobody else has been sneaking calls." After a brief pause, he continued: "Or maybe the group wants to set a precedent that it's O.K. for one of its members to do it and that it's O.K. to form a conspiracy to cover it up. After all, if one can do it and get away with it, so can you. So, if any of you know about another group member sneaking calls and don't say anything, it's really because you want to be able to do the same thing. You can B.S. yourself about it, too, saying it's no big deal. But here's how it really works: You start out with just a minor rule violation or two and cover it up, and then it's just a little way to the next bigger one. Before you know it, it'll be O.K. to drink and use on the unit." After another pause, someone finally spoke up.

"I know someone else who's been sneaking phone calls. " Tom said gravely.

"And I suppose he's been wanting you to cover up for him, hasn't he, Tom?" the therapist asked. "That'd be like covering up for somebody who's having a heart attack. He'd wind up dead anyway, and you'd be sicker because of the guilt and because of lying for him. Do you think he's going to get honest, or is he going to force you to name him?"

After another long, uncomfortable pause, Mel bailed out Tom by confessing, "It's me," and then he detailed the story of the secret phone calls he had been making to his mistress.

The therapist processed this confession briefly, asked if there were any others, and, hearing none, proceeded to narrow the line of inquiry further. "Now, what are some *other* ways that an addict might put his love interest ahead of his recovery? Something other than phone calls."

"How about sneaking a visit," Paul proposed.

"Yeah, how about sneaking a visit," the therapist repeated. "That's a good one. A real sick, good one. A real sick, dishonest, good one." Out of the corner of his eye, the therapist could see George blushing and moving uncomfortably in his chair. "He'd have to be a real sick bastard to sneak a visit outside of visiting hours, wouldn't he Paul?"

"I guess so," ventured Paul.

"A sick addict who'd sneak a visit like that had better have a good time, because he'd be risking his own recovery and the recovery of every other person in the group. He'd better have a *merry* good time," the therapist emphasized, drawing out the word "merry," which sounds just like "Mary," who is the girlfriend George had been visiting.

George tried to speak, but the therapist interrupted him. "Not now, George, I'm talking to Paul." Then, looking back at Paul, "Tell me, just who would a sick addict like that be likely to visit?"

Paul answered, "Maybe his wife or a girlfriend."

"A *girlfriend*. A wife or a *girlfriend*. That makes sense," the therapist asserted. Then, George tried to speak again, now looking visibly upset. The therapist noticed, and, speaking as if to a misbehaving child, said: "George, I told you I was talking to Paul. Now, what is it?"

At last, George confessed. The therapist then led a group discussion on what specific measures the group was going to take in order to deal with its problem of members who had been sneaking phone calls and visits.

This vignette illustrates not only backward communication, but several sub-techniques and/or helpful hints that assist the implementation of backward communication and are often useful in their own right in influencing group process.

First, the therapist involved as many different patients in the process as possible by spreading his questions around. Most groups are dominated by a few verbal members, while shy, bashful patients rarely speak spontaneously. This technique gets the quiet ones to open up and helps them learn needed social skills, while at the same time serving a group level function by changing the process from domination by the few to one in which all the members participate.

Another technique designed to maximize participation by all members was that of looking at one patient while asking a question, then abruptly switching and expecting the answer from a different patient (in this illustration, looking at Bob, then calling on Frank). Once the group witnessed this technique, all group members were forced to be ready with an answer to every question, since each member might be called on unexpectedly, regardless of whom the therapist seemed to be addressing at any given moment. Another way of describing this maneuver is to say that it heightened response-attentiveness.

Participation can also be enhanced by the technique of labeling nonparticipation as sick. Since all patients said that they were in treatment to recover, and recovery had to come first (here are those previously established principles again), it was inconsistent with their own stated goals to sit silently without raising hands or to refuse to identify a patient who had been sneaking phone calls. The therapist had only to remind them of their stated goals, point out the inconsistency, and characterize their failure to pursue their own goals as irresponsibility, which is a major symptom of addiction. That left members with only two choices: either go along with the therapist's directive to participate or refuse and risk being identified as more distinctly and dramatically sick.

The therapist used the format to teach the group about addiction and principles of recovery by utilizing ongoing patient behavior as examples of the ideas he felt the group needed to learn. When a patient's answer to a question indicated that the patient understood an important concept, the therapist positively reinforced it by agreeing, saying "Good," or similar responses. When a patient's answer indicated misunderstanding or a "sick" attitude, the therapist negatively reinforced it by disagreeing or labeling it as sick, and then explained the applicable concept or principle. The backward communication process of progressing from general categories to specific examples has the effect of teaching how specific target behaviors actually relate to addiction and recovery, so that patients do not see the target behaviors in isolation and conclude that they are just "bad."

Just as nightclub entertainers must learn to handle hecklers and drunks in the audience, a therapist must be prepared to deal with resistant, resentful alcoholics and addicts who may adopt the role of critic, consumer advocate, anarchist, or other type of agitator. Such rebels' objections are usually irrational and aim more to disrupt the group or to embarrass or discredit the therapist (or other group members), rather than to attempt to bring about constructive change; therefore, the rebels cannot be reasoned out of their objections. The best method is to label them quickly as sick and irrational, and then dismiss them, as the therapist did with Fred. The therapist also talked about, rather than directly to, Fred, which made it impossible for Fred to engage the therapist in a pointless and time-wasting argument.

A similar approach, not seen in the example above, is to encourage rebels to convert their complaints into suggestions for changing the program, and then to point out how ludicrous it is for them to attempt to manage their treatment when they cannot even manage their own lives. A therapist once made a motion in a Patient Government meeting, which carried, to the effect that, by a certain date, the group would fill a slotted cardboard box with written "program improvement suggestions." On the designated morning, the patients ceremoniously handed the box to the therapist, who then immediately jumped out of his seat and walked briskly to the nearest trash can, where he pulled all the written suggestions out of the box and dumped them, without even looking at them, as he delivered a loud and abrasive diatribe about how unmanageable the lives of alcoholics and addicts are, and how they are affected by the symptoms of grandiosity and impaired judgment.

Another technique visible in the backward communication vignette was that of involving patients affectively as well as cognitively. Recovery from addiction must be emotional as well as intellectual. Patients need to learn to deal with powerful emotions without having to drink or use over them, and one way to teach them to do that is to continually arouse powerful emotions in them in a supportive setting. The therapist aroused anger, guilt, and anxiety throughout the example.

One technique for arousing anger was to use veiled or indirect insults, or insults directed at the group as a whole ("What would you think of a blankety-blank S.O.B. who would do a dirty rotten, sick, dishonest, cowardly thing like that?" or "This group is killing Joe!"), delivered in an abrasive, sarcastic tone. Although the therapist was careful never to verbally abuse or use profanity on any patient directly, he did *sound* verbally abusive and profane, and patients often took his manner personally and became angry. Patients also became angry when the therapist talked about them in their presence, the way parents often discuss their children in their presence. Finally, the therapist frequently (though not necessarily in the present example) made reference or alluded to issues the population of patients was likely to be emotionally sensitive about, such as the issue of cowardice in a population of veterans, or the issue of homosexuality in a population of men—some of whom had been subjected to homosexual behavior in prison.

Another method for arousing affective responses is the diatribe. The therapist often "got up on the soap box" to decry a group behavior (such as enabling) or a social problem (such as society's encouraging drinking but punishing alcoholics). Depending on whether group members agreed with his diatribe, they became angry or guilty, fired up or ashamed. Often, the therapist delivered the diatribe as a stern lecture designed to arouse old, stored-up antipathy toward arrogant or inequitable authority figures, which could then be processed with peers to relieve resentment and heal over festering emotional sores.

Finally, the therapist attempted to build suspense and tension through pacing. Just as a good Hitchcock thriller could bring moviegoers to the "edges of their seats," a well-timed series of interventions by a therapist could arouse considerable emotion.

Once a group had been through a backward communication session, members knew immediately that the therapist was "zeroing in" on something or someone as soon as he asked a question like "What are we here for?" or "How might an addict rip off a treatment program?" From that moment, the dramatic tension begins to build, and the therapist can enhance it by seeming to aim in one direction, then back off, then seeming to go in another direction, and so on, until most members of the group find their fists clenched and their bodies dripping with sweat. The feeling in the air is similar to what people might experience knowing that a giant is approaching, and hearing the thundering footsteps growing louder and louder. Often, this tension is the primary cause of confessions by members who tell what they did just to "get it over with."

When patients seemed ready to confess, as with George, the therapist often delayed them, and this tactic was capable of leading them to confess "harder," or to confess more than they might have confessed had they been allowed to confess on the first try. The fact that the therapist *allowed* them to confess, instead of demanding it, is the essence of backward communication. Frustrating or delaying the confessions enhanced the overall effectiveness of the technique.

Another factor related to confessions is the power that progressing from the general to the specific has in eliciting unexpected confessions of behaviors similar to the target behavior, which were committed by patients other than the one or ones the therapist had in mind. When the behavior being discussed is still too general for members to be able to guess the target behavior, many group members begin to wonder if the process is being directed at them. When the tension mounts, they confess. This tendency has, more than once, brought to light serious problems that the treatment staff would never have known about otherwise.

Backward communication is a very versatile technique because it can be used in so many different situations. Another time it was used occurred when treatment staff discovered that patients in a hospital-based program, where only decaffeinated coffee was allowed, had smuggled in regular coffee and placed it in one of the cans marked "decaffeinated." An older patient was overheard whispering to a newcomer about which container held "the good stuff." Neither patient grasped that, although they were only talking about caffeine, the interaction followed the same pattern that it would have followed if they had smuggled in and whispered about cocaine, alcohol, or any other drug. A therapist held a group session that day in which a backward communication was set up with smuggling caffeine as the bullseye and smuggling drugs in general as one of the outer rings.

The technique found use in a classroom as well. During a class on chemical dependency counseling skills, the teacher discovered that one of the students had plagiarized some material for his term paper. He decided to use the incident to demonstrate backward communication to the class. First, he asked the class how important it was for them to be positive role models for their patients and clients; then he asked for examples of ways they might be poor role models. When one of them mentioned dishonesty, he asked for examples of that. As they came up with examples, he asked more specifically about how they might be dishonest in the class. Finally, when a student brought up plagiarism, the teacher stopped the process to spare the plagiarist public humiliation, and explained to the class what he had been doing. Interestingly, he found that some members he had not suspected of plagiarism were ready to confess—even some who had merely used quotations liberally in their papers and had attributed the quotations properly to their sources.

SACRIFICES

A group sacrifices when it decides to give up something in order to show love and concern for a single patient (or, on occasion, for several patients, or even for the entire group). It is a constructive alternative to punishment when a group member has behaved irresponsibly or violated a rule or an established group principle. For example, if the group discovers that the coffee-making area is messy, the entire group might sacrifice coffee for 24 hours in the name of the person who is responsible for keeping the area clean, instead of punishing that individual.

The idea of sacrificing is well grounded in Alcoholics Anonymous principles relating to recovery. The A.A. book, *Twelve Steps and Twelve Traditions*, states in the very first sentence of its discussion of Tradition Twelve: "The spiritual substance of anonymity is sacrifice" (page 184). The book, which is the closest thing available to a definitive statement of what A.A. is all about, repeatedly reinforces the theme that willingness to "give up personal desires for the common good" is an important foundation for the A.A. way of life.

When a group decides to sacrifice, it needs to make the decision voluntarily, because a sacrifice is a willing, loving giving up of something by a group of peers. If the staff were to require the group to make a sacrifice, it would not be a sacrifice as defined here; it would be punishment by authority and not unlike the kind of discipline employed by drill instructors in military basic training, in which the entire group suffers for the misdeeds of an individual. This type of discipline is capable of mobilizing group pressure and focusing it on an individual, but, because it is punishment imposed by authority, it tends to arouse hostility, both in the individual and in the group. A true sacrifice, done correctly, arouses guilt in the individual and offers the group a concrete, constructive measure that it can employ to "do something" about its member's misbehavior.

When people break rules in the "real world," they expect to be singled out and punished if caught, or—if the authority in charge of their discipline is ignorant about the negative effects of doing so—to be "chewed out" or "called on the carpet," and then given one more chance. When a group sacrifices, violators instead face a group of peers who willingly suffer for them. Violators then feel both guilt about causing an entire group to suffer and secure and valued because of the group's willingness to do something for them. The whole tone of discipline is changed by the use of this technique. It causes resistant, manipulative patients to become very cooperative and responsible, and therefore more open to the possibility of recovery.

Sacrifices can be very colorful, dramatic experiences, which help patients to accumulate "recovery memories" that are as interesting as their drinking or drug-using memories. Sacrifices can also involve patients in doing things they would not ordinarily do that by themselves are supportive of recovery. For example, many patients suffer great fear of "looking like a fool" in public, which causes them to reach for a little "liquid (or chemical) courage" at the prospect appearing foolish. Such patients benefit greatly from learning to tolerate mild embarrassment without having to drink or use drugs to do it. The best way to learn this kind of lesson is to live through an embarrassing ordeal. Milton Erickson created many therapeutic ordeals for his patients, and Jay Haley authored an entire book, *Ordeal Therapy* (1984), about the process.

Shortly after a new treatment program was established, groups began to carry out sacrifices. The earliest ones were simple and, though inconvenient, not particularly painful. The first things to go were smoking and drinking coffee in meetings, at first for a day at a time, then a week, and then longer, as the group struggled to manage the behavior of its members under the scrutiny of the staff, who continually discovered new "alcoholic behaviors" and irresponsibilities, and demanded that the group do something about them. Eventually, the group gave up smoking and drinking coffee during groups *forever*. Television and video games suffered a similar fate, eventually also to be banished forever. Finally, the group reached a point where it required great creativity in order to come up with new ways to sacrifice:

The Patient Government was debating what it was going to do about a member who had earlier confessed to an irresponsible, addictive behavior as the result of the therapist's use of backward communication. The group was frustrated, because there seemed to be nothing left for it to sacrifice, and it appeared to be desperate for a suggestion from the therapist so that it could make a decision quickly and then go on to other business. In a flash of creativity, the therapist suggested that the group gather in the hospital lobby and sing "Call Me Irresponsible." The offending member would not be required to sing, but would have to go along and watch. The motion seemed so zany that the group was caught off guard and carried it swiftly.

The therapist located a copy of sheet music containing the words and the tune, photocopied it, and distributed it to the patients. The next morning, the group gathered in the lobby to carry out the motion. During the report to the Patient Government meeting afterward, the chairman described the antics of what he humorously called "the cherry nose choir." He began by voicing his opinion that the sounds emanating from the group more closely resembled caterwauling than singing, and the tune was barely recognizable. He continued, pointing out that, when the song was done, the group briefly stood in silence. That was when he and other group members noticed the people who had been sitting in the lobby, witnessing this musical display. They appeared confused, looking first at the group and then at each other, wondering how they should respond. Finally, one man began to clap. Soon, he was joined by others, until all were applauding approvingly.

Before the sacrifice, as the time approached for the group to sing, most members were filled with dread at the thought of how embarrassed they would feel. After the event, which had been placed in an entirely different light by the approving reaction of the "audience," most members felt a good deal less fearful of embarrassing moments or situations, and more confident of their ability to weather them.

This sacrifice, and many like it, taught hundreds of alcoholics and addicts that embarrassment was not fatal and could be made much more tolerable if it were leavened with humor. A similar sacrifice, described below, led to a minor restriction of program activities, but it was effective at the time and lived on for years in the memories of many former patients and staff as the quintessential outrageous sacrifice:

Just before the Patient Government meeting, a nurse told the therapist that wet towels and other debris had been found on the floor of the communal shower. The therapist used this information to conduct a backward communication session beginning with the importance of responsibility in recovery, narrowing down to a definition of responsibility as cleaning up one's own messes, and eventually leading to confessions by several group members about having left the shower room in disarray.

Next, the therapist demanded that the group do something about its irresponsibility, and the familiar chaos and indecision ensued. After a prolonged period of debate, the group finally voted to carry the therapist's motion that the group would go collectively to the duck pond at noon the next day, wearing turbans fashioned from towels on their heads, and quack the tune of "Call Me Irresponsible" to the ducks. The group carried out the sacrifice and experienced the usual therapeutic benefits.

Unfortunately, the timing was wrong for this sacrifice, because a number of visiting dignitaries were on the grounds at noon, along with numerous visitors and lunchgoers. The incident led to an inquiry by the hospital administration, which resulted in the program's having to confine future singing sacrifices to the unit. In addition, the program developed a reputation in some quarters as "that place where they quack at the ducks." In spite of all this "negative press," the patients felt good about the experience and believed that it enhanced their recoveries while giving them a fun experience to remember.

One more example of a sacrifice is given, to demonstrate how

sacrifices can be used experientially to teach the Ninth Step of
A.A., ("Made direct amends . . ."):

One morning, the therapist arrived on the unit and discovered a nearby grocery store's shopping cart sitting in the din-
ing room. Patients routinely made "runs" to this store for
cigarettes and other necessities and had apparently "bor-
rowed" a cart to ease the job of carrying their purchases. He
said nothing about the discovery until the Patient
Government meeting, where he led a discussion beginning
with the importance of honesty in recovery; continuing with
examples of dishonesty, including the fact that felony theft
was a flagrant example of dishonesty; and culminating in the
group's having to take some action about its crime of shopping cart theft.

After much discussion, the group decided to return the
cart, apologize in person to the store manager, and collect
and bring into the store all shopping carts they could find
in the parking lot. The therapist urged the gesture of bringing in the carts as an amend, because "Step Nine doesn't say
'Made direct apologies.' It says: 'Made direct amends.' You
need to *do* something to make up for the crime you committed. To just apologize would be like robbing a bank and then
going back and saying, 'I'm sorry I robbed your bank,' but
keeping the money."

The following day, the leader of the amend brigade gave
his report: "When we got to the store, I went inside to
look for the manager. I was hoping the manager wasn't
there, and I asked a guy who didn't look important if he
knew where the manager was. He said that he *was* the manager. That was when I felt like sinking into a hole in the
floor. Well, there I was, stuck. So I told him we were a
group of alcoholics from the hospital and that we had bor-
rowed one of his carts. I said that when we realized that
borrowing his cart was stealing, we brought it back, and
several of us were outside bringing in carts from the park-

ing lot to make up for it. Just then, the doors opened on both sides of the store, and the other guys were pushing long lines of carts through the doors. When the manager saw that, his jaw dropped, and he said: 'You guys can borrow a cart from this store any time.'"

UTILIZATION

Utilization techniques were described in the last chapter, as they are applied to individuals. Now, the subject turns to utilization as it is applied at the group process level. In order to employ a utilization technique at this level, the therapist needs to be attuned to the behavior of the group as an entity, while also attending to the behavior of the individuals in it. Then, from this dual-level perspective, the therapist can utilize whatever the group is doing in order to influence group decisions and actions.

The primary group-level behavior or behavior tendency that therapists must attend to is whether a group is cooperating with or rebelling against their suggestions. In addition, it is important to pick up the predominant affective tone of a group, which, with chemically dependent groups, is most likely to be one of the following: anger, guilt, fear or anxiety, impatience, stubborn willfulness, confusion, or loving concern. When therapists can tell which way a group is "leaning," they can either utilize that tendency as it is or intervene to enhance it first and then utilize it.

For example, if a group is cooperative, therapists can influence its decisions and behavior easily, simply by suggesting that the group do what they suggest. (If a therapist has gotten the group to adopt the principle that the group will responsibly carry out its decisions, then the therapist's task is simplified: all the therapist needs to do to influence group behavior is to influence group decisions. Then, the group's decision, or promise to behave a certain way, is likely to translate directly into its carrying out that behavior.)

If a group is not only cooperative, but also guilty, therapists can enhance the group's cooperativeness further by utilizing or playing on the guilt. To do this, therapists need only remind the group of its awesome responsibility and what *could* happen if its decision is not made carefully; remind the group of its own faulty or harmful past decisions; or remind members of their collective past misdeeds, such as their having cheated employers, endangered others while driving under the influence, or abused their spouses or children. Then, with the group's guilt aroused and floating palpably in the air, therapists can push for the most therapeutically desirable decision by tying the guilt to the appropriate side of the issue being considered, in such a way that the group will expect that making the decision in the preferred direction will reduce its guilt.

Cooperative groups are easy to influence, but the real challenge is finding a way to influence rebellious, resistant groups. This task is especially challenging when groups are not only resistant but angry. Without utilization techniques, therapists might feel that they are being "eaten alive" by such groups. Alcoholics and addicts seem to have a knack for finding people's emotional Achilles' heels—probably because they have needed to develop this ability for self-protection or to make it easier to "con" others. This ability makes it possible for an aroused group of addicts to deeply wound a therapist. With utilization techniques, therapists can not only survive such groups, but powerfully influence even the most angry and resistant ones.

The key is to accept and utilize the anger and resistance. Therapists can accept the anger by being attuned to when a group is trying to probe them to find a flaw to exploit. For example, groups of addicts typically ask new therapists in a challenging manner if the therapists are recovering alcoholics or addicts themselves. If therapists admit they are not, the groups then label the therapists as being incapable of understanding or helping them. Therapists are much better off being evasive or refusing to answer such questions, and then firing back questions of their own, such as: "If you've just had a heart attack, and you're about to die unless the emergency room doctor gets your heart started, would you tell everyone to wait a minute while you find out if the doctor has ever had a heart attack? Or refuse to allow any doctor who has not had a heart attack to work on you? Or, as you're going down for the third time, would you pause to inquire whether the lifeguard who just swam out to save you has ever almost drowned?"

Another way to accept a group's hostile probing for flaws is to provide the group with a bunch of good made-up flaws before the group is able to find any real ones. For example, therapists can admit that they received their degrees from unaccredited Caribbean colleges, that they are complete impostors, that they are not alcoholics or addicts and do not even know what alcohol tastes like, that they are mentally ill, that they are homosexual, or whatever the group might find "juicy" and useful in disqualifying the therapist. Therapists can either immediately admit to flaws that are obviously and outrageously false or start out sounding believable and innocent for awhile, then build on their stories until their absurdity is apparent to everyone.

It is actually fairly simple to utilize resistance and anger in a group. When a therapist wants a group to choose Decision A over Decision B, the therapist can often get an angry, rebellious group to choose Decision A by simply insisting on Decision B. Sometimes, a group is rebellious but guilty, or rebellious but not quite rebellious enough to do the opposite of what the therapist wants. In this case, the therapist needs to build up the anger first, then take a strong stand in the opposite direction of the desired decision.

To carry off this sort of strategy, a therapist needs to be constantly aware of which way the group's "wind" is blowing. Therapists can accomplish this by constantly making suggestions and offering proposals. In a parliamentarily run group, the therapist can accomplish this by frequently making motions. Each time the group reacts to a suggestion, the therapist has a reading of the group's tendencies.

A resistant, angry group can be made more resistant and angry if the therapist addresses it in a sarcastic, insulting manner, or rants, raves, and lectures, or plays dirty tricks. An example of a dirty trick is the time a therapist made the accusation in a Patient Government meeting that a member of the group had a bottle of alcohol in his room—an accusation that the group quickly denied. The therapist dared the group to prove that it was telling the truth by agreeing to do a sacrifice chosen by the therapist, without knowing in advance what the sacrifice might be, if there was, in fact, a bottle of alcohol in a patient's room. The group accepted the dare and voted to carry out whatever sacrifice the therapist chose if there were a bottle of alcohol in a patient's room. The therapist then led the entire group to a patient's room, where he pointed out a bottle of aftershave—a bottle, the group was forced to admit, that contained alcohol. Finally, the therapist announced a decidedly unpleasant and inconvenient sacrifice. Needless to say, the group was quite vexed by this interchange, especially when the therapist pointed out how irresponsible it would be for the group to try to get out of its commitment. The therapist enhanced the anger further by arrogantly pointing out how easy it was to "con a bunch of cons," and how unmanageable their lives obviously were.

Therapists can often tune into a group's *rhythm* of resistance and utilize the fluctuations to influence group process. Changes in the level of resistance may seem random, with the group being resistant one moment, compliant the next, and something else a moment later. Sometimes, however, the changes are predictable. They often occur as reactions to decisions that the group has just made and has second thoughts or feelings about. For example, a group may compliantly but grudgingly pass a motion that the therapist strongly advocated, and then, reacting to feeling it had been pushed, become quite resistant about the next suggestion the therapist makes. The therapist can often take advantage of this change by advocating at that moment a position opposite to what he or she really wants. Conversely, after a group defies a therapist and defeats a motion the therapist argued in favor of, it often becomes guilty—especially if the therapist anticipates the guilt and magnifies it—and will then pass almost any motion the therapist suggests, even if the motion is to vote down the previous motion.

Therapists can always utilize groups' tendency to people-please to push through desired decisions, but with certain cautions. Actually, people-pleasing in this context is usually less about pleasing someone than it is about getting someone else to make the decision, so that the people-pleaser does not have to feel responsible. Groups will often make decisions that therapists seem to want the groups to make, simply to pass responsibility for the decision to the therapists. Therapists can utilize this tendency as a shortcut to get favorable group decisions made, but they must take additional steps to ensure that the group accepts responsibility for its decision. Often, it is enough to remind groups of previous principles they have accepted.

Therapists can also force people-pleasing groups to accept responsibility for their decisions by being impossible to please. They can do this by alternately supporting opposite choices. Just as the group is about to adopt the decision the therapist has been advocating, the therapist begins to argue for the opposite decision. When the group changes its mind and is ready to go in the new direction, the therapist reverts to the old position. A skilled therapist can keep the resultant "creative chaos" going for quite a long time, until the group's frustration and anxiety about time constraints reach a critical point. Then, the therapist can utilize these reactions and "allow" the group to finally decide. Which particular moment the therapist chooses to relent and let the group decide—now with full responsibility for its choice, because it is not basing its decision on whether the therapist is pleased—generally determines which decision the group makes. All the therapist needs to do is wait until the pendulum has swung in the desired direction before giving up and letting the group decide.

Although this chapter's focus is on utilizing group behavior, some individually focused utilization that was done in one treatment program is worthy of description, because it became institutionalized as a practice of the group, and therapists employed it constantly in group sessions. One of the "rules" for therapists in that program was to utilize everything.

For example, a resistant patient who appeared for treatment with a plaster cast on his broken leg soon found the group voting to write the Twelve Steps on the cast, instead of the usual autographs one finds on casts. Much to this patient's chagrin, both because he did not want to admit his alcoholism and because he was a perfectionist about grammar, one of the appointed writers added the phrase: "I am a alcoholic."

Another example was the assignment of the two private, one-person rooms on the unit, a decision the group was responsible for making. Therapists realized that the group would probably want to assign the private rooms as rewards to politically astute and powerful group members, thus creating a form of class differentiation and countertherapeutic favoritism. The presence of these rooms could have been perceived as a problem, but the therapists decided to *utilize* them instead.

They redefined, or reframed, the purpose of the rooms and called them "isolation rooms." They urged the group to assign to these rooms only those patients who were dangerous to the other patients, who were sick to the point of being "contagious." The group agreed with this definition, and each time patients were assigned to one of the rooms, they received a powerful, denial-smashing message about their disease. Later, the staff took over the task of room assignment, because group decisions were slow and unwieldy, and room assignments had to be made on admission. The meaning of assignment to private rooms stuck, however, and patients dreaded being placed in them.

OFFERING SEVERAL ALTERNATIVES, ANY OF WHICH IS ACCEPTABLE

It is possible for a therapist to ensure that a group will make decisions in the desired direction by presenting the group with a range of alternatives that includes only decisions that are acceptable to the therapist. This technique was devised originally as a permissive method for overcoming resistance to direct, authoritarian hypnotic suggestions. Rather than being told exactly what to do, a patient is given a choice, and this perception (or illusion) of being able to choose meets the patient's need to feel self-directed. Here is an example:

Al's discharge date had been set when he was admitted, and it was coming up soon. In fact, the therapist and group were sitting in the last Patient Government meeting before Al was to go home, and the group was responsible for setting and changing discharge dates; therefore, this was the last chance for the group to decide whether Al should be discharged as planned or have his stay extended. Just the day before, Al had presented his Discharge Plan. Both the meager contents of the plan and his lackadaisical attitude while presenting it had demonstrated convincingly, at least in the minds of the therapist and of the healthier and more perceptive group members, that Al had only the foggiest idea of what his problems were and had no grasp whatsoever of what he needed to do in order to stay sober.

The therapist knew that Al was not ready to be discharged, but he also knew that there was some resistance in the group to extending Al's stay in the hospital. Because of their own denial and poor grasp of the seriousness of addiction in general and of Al's addiction in particular, some group members believed that Al was actually ready to go. Al, being in denial, believed along with these group members that he was ready for discharge, and he very much wanted to leave. Therefore, he had taken advantage of the fact that he was popular with his peers and had done some politicking in an effort to collect votes in favor of letting him go home on his original discharge date.

The therapist considered using the technique of offering several alternatives, any of which is acceptable, by asking the group whether Al's stay should be extended for two weeks or for a month. This way, he would lead the group to focus on *how long* to extend Al's stay, instead of on *whether* or not to do so. Upon reflection, the therapist discarded this idea, because the group had already been led, by Al's politicking, to question whether his stay should be extended. Someone was bound to bring up that alternative, which would undermine the strategy. Therefore, the therapist decided to modify the approach and present two different alternatives: Either extend Al's stay or discharge him immediately. The first alternative was what the therapist preferred for the group to do, while the second was close to what Al and the sicker members wanted, but with a modification that made it acceptable to the therapist—to discharge him *before* his discharge date and thereby deprive him of a sanctioned graduation. The therapist told the group: "Do you want to extend him until he's ready to go or do you want to throw him out *now*, because he's hopeless?"

The therapist then argued for the second alternative, both to demonstrate that he found it acceptable and to prevent the group from discharging Al only because it was resistant toward the therapist (that is, discharging him only because it believed the therapist wanted Al to stay): "I think you ought to give up on him, wash your hands of him. Don't even wait until tomorrow. Get him out *now*. I would understand. After all, nobody likes to be reminded of their failures. Nobody wants somebody hanging around to make them think of how serious their disease is or of how irresponsible the group has been with him. Besides, you're not your brother's keepers. Why shouldn't you give up on him like everyone else has, or will? Sure, you could extend him. But I like the idea of throwing him out now. Then, the group will have to live with what it's done. And after he's gone, I'll make it my business to remind you every day of how you killed him. Let's go. Let's get him out. I make a motion that Al be escorted to the door immediately as a hopeless drunk."

The group began to struggle. No group member could argue for discharging Al immediately without resembling the therapist's parody (or seeming to be the therapist's "yesman"). That alternative seemed too extreme and too unsafe. Some members began to argue in favor of letting Al stay until his discharge date, as planned, but the therapist refused to allow that alternative: "Why wait? What difference will one day make? If you think he's ready tomorrow, then he's ready now, so just go ahead and throw the bum out. If you don't have the heart to do that, then extend him and give him the help he needs. There aren't any other real choices. You'll either help him or you'll give up on him. Come on, let's vote. There's a motion on the floor."

The motion died for lack of a second. Then, the group began to discuss extending Al's stay. That was the only alternative left. Al argued, saying he was ready to be discharged and he was going to leave anyway. The therapist backed up all of Al's arguments, but in an exaggerated, crazy way that made them all seem sick, which helped push the momentum in the direction of the extension.

As it became apparent that the group was going to vote for an extension, the therapist became concerned about how long the group would extend Al's stay. He feared that the group would compromise with Al and settle for a short extension, such as a week or less, which would not be long enough to benefit Al. Therefore, he chose this point to employ the original strategy, and he asked the group whether it wanted to extend him for two weeks or for a month.

The group settled on two weeks, and Al announced that he was going to leave anyway. The therapist suggested that Al was on a dry drunk. Al protested in such an exaggerated manner that the group was forced to agree with the therapist and then voted to place Al on detox watch for 24 hours. When Al refused to put on his pajamas, the group decided that all other members would wear their pajamas until he put on his. Al finally relented, put on his pajamas, and decided to stay the two additional weeks. During the extended stay, Al presented a much improved revised Discharge Plan and left the hospital with a considerably higher chance of continued sobriety than he would have had if he had left on schedule.

ENCOURAGING OR PREDICTING RESISTANCE

In the last chapter, the use of this technique with individuals was described at length. As with the above technique, one can also transfer this easily from an individual to a group setting by addressing the group as an entity and encouraging it to do the opposite of what one wants it to do, or predicting that it will do what one wants it not to do. It can also work at both the individual and group levels simultaneously, as in the following example:

Bud Smith had been extremely resistant and hostile during his entire two weeks in the program. He had been a rather peripheral group member and seemed contemptuous of treatment staff. He appeared to be in danger of failing to bond with the group and, as a result, perhaps leaving against medical advice or eloping. Since time alone had not brought Bud closer to his peers or made him more open to working at his recovery, the therapist decided that a more active intervention was necessary very soon.

The therapist watched Bud out of the corner of his eye. Before long, just as expected, Bud uttered a disparaging comment under his breath, showing his disdain for the therapeutic process. The therapist turned toward Bud, leaned forward in his chair, curled his lip into an exaggerated sneer, pointed dramatically toward the door, and shouted: "Hey, Smith: If you don't like it here, Get out!" This was the first move of an intervention aimed at getting Bud more strongly invested in treatment by aligning him with the group against the therapist and then influencing the group to unite around him.

Bud looked shocked. All eyes were on the therapist, then on Bud. Almost inaudibly, Bud asked, "What?"

"You heard me. GET OUT!" the therapist intoned, even more loudly than the first time. He continued, sounding almost unbelievably arrogant, domineering, and sarcastic: "You don't want to be here. You don't want to recover. You're wasting my time, you're wasting the group's time, and you're wasting your own time. Why would you want to sit in here when you could be out drinking? Why don't you get honest and go out and tie on a good one? Huh? Go on! GET OUT!"

Bud's facial expression transformed several times and finally settled on stubborn. He crossed his arms defiantly. "You're not getting *me* out of here."

"Oh yeah?" asked the therapist. "We'll see about that." He turned to address the entire group: "I want this guy out of here and I want him out now. Since he's too yellow bellied to walk out on his own, I'm going to *force* you to *throw* him out. I make a motion that the group throw Smith out on the bricks—NOW!"

No one would second the motion. The therapist's glaring eyes swept back and forth over the group. Finally, he urged: "Come on. What's the matter with you guys? Isn't anybody going to second my motion? I dare you." Finally, one patient accepted the dare. The Chairman called the motion to a vote, and only the therapist's hand rose in favor. The vote against was overwhelming. "Well," the therapist admitted, "I guess I know when I've been beat."

The therapist in this example knew that he was taking a risk by instructing a patient to "get out." But the risk was less than it would ordinarily have been, because the group had repeatedly responded to members' walking out of treatment by following them, in one case all the way outside to his car, and making every

effort to talk them into coming back. Besides, the risk of elope-
ment was much higher for those who left stealthily, in the night,
than it was for those who left publicly and dramatically. If a patient
chooses the middle of a group session to walk out, it is likely that
he or she probably wants to be talked into staying, or at least has
mixed motives.

PROVIDING A WORSE ALTERNATIVE

This tactic also makes the transition easily from an individual
to a group setting. It consists of asking or demanding a behavior
of a patient or group which is an extreme member of a class of
behaviors, where the behavior the therapist desires is a less
extreme member of the same class. This approach allows the
patient or group to satisfy any need there may be to resist the therapist's suggestion, but it leads the patient or group subtly to consider other members of the same class of behaviors, and often to
"spontaneously" carry out one of them.

For example, the kind of interaction that occurred in the
vignette just before the one above, in which the group voted to
extend Al's stay in treatment, happened on almost a daily basis
in groups held in that setting. Often, groups were cooperative
about extending patients' stays, but became resistant on the subject
of how long to extend them. The technique of providing a worse
alternative was very helpful in leading the group to approve extensions of adequate duration.

The group was just finishing its last item of business
before considering whether and for how long to extend
Slim's stay in the program. The group was obviously in
favor of an extension, but Slim had been pressuring for a
short extension, claiming his boss—who had been
attending family sessions and was strongly supportive of
treatment—might fire him if he stayed more than one
extra week (an obviously false concern). The treatment

team felt that Slim needed at least two weeks longer, perhaps a month, and felt certain that the boss would
approve. The therapist raised his hand and said: "I move
that Slim be extended for 90 days."

Slim was too shocked to speak at first. Another group
member spoke up on his behalf, arguing that Slim was sure
to lose his job if he stayed that long. The therapist countered:
"What good is a job to a stiff?" Then, parodying the fact that
the other patient had spoken up for Slim, he continued: "I
see Slim has had an attorney appointed to represent him in
this hearing. Well, I want the group—and Slim's counsel—to
consider that Slim is just too damn sick to leave any sooner
than 90 days."

The discussion continued, with arguments going back
and forth on both sides. Finally, the therapist "settled" for
an extension of three weeks. Slim breathed a heavy sigh,
relieved that he had avoided a 90-day extension.

Here is a variation of the same technique used in a similar
situation:

The therapist felt that the group was not accepting how seriously addicted and impaired Dick was. He waited until the
group was addressing some issue that was entirely unrelated
to Dick and raised his hand to say: "I make a motion that
Dick be extended for six months." Dick and other members
objected, saying that Dick's planned discharge date was not
even close and that Dick had not even begun his Discharge
Plan. The therapist argued back that those things did not
matter, because Dick was so sick that the group did not have
to hear his Discharge Plan to know that he needed to stay
longer.

Finally, even though the group seemed ready to vote in
favor of an extension, the therapist backed down and with-
drew his motion. Later, when Dick's discharge date was near,
the group extended his stay by a month. In the meantime,

the group was more aware of Dick's need for extra help and provided it, by, among other things, electing Dick to be Chairman.

This technique was effective in other situations besides questions of whether or for how long to extend patients' stays. For example, therapists often urged groups to perform outrageous sacrifices that they knew the group would refuse to go along with, but which made lesser sacrifices in the same direction seem much less unattractive by comparison. One suggestion that groups always rejected was that all members shave their heads. Although patients never lost the hair from their heads, several groups voted to shave mustaches or beards, or to give up shaving their faces for a period of time. One therapist liked to add humor by suggesting the "compromise" of just shaving *half* their heads.

CONFUSION-RESTRUCTURING

Just as a person becomes more open to suggestions when confused and off balance, so does a group. Neither a person nor a group finds confusion particularly pleasant, and either will seek out clarifying information or be extraordinarily open to clarifying suggestions at the peak of confusion and disorientation.

One of the primary functions of one treatment program was to induce confusion in both patients and groups, and then resolve the confusion by providing Twelve Step, Alcoholics Anonymous information. Gradually, as the cycle of confusion-restructuring was repeated over and over, patients and groups became more and more accepting of A.A. ideas and principles.

It is relatively easy to induce confusion. Alcoholics and addicts are confused and disoriented initially when they arrive in treatment by a combination of factors, including being in a new place with strange rules and customs, the effects of drug and alcohol withdrawal, and residual cognitive impairment. Then, they are faced with a situation where they, as members of a group, are entirely responsible for their own treatment and the treatment of their peers, with no clear guidance or instruction on how to be so.

The dilemma of being in charge of all clinical decisions without being told what to do creates a powerful drive in groups for information about how to act. Many group sessions feel like a game of "hide and seek," in which the groups try every imaginable angle to get the therapists to tell them what to do and therapists manage to be obscure about what decision the groups should make, while being clear that it is the groups' responsibility to decide.

Often, group members directly asked therapists what to do. Therapists responded with statements like: "Do the right thing." When pressed to further elucidate such answers, therapists provided such unenlightening explanations as: "Do what you know is best," or "The right decision is the one that's best for everyone."

Patients' impaired cognitive processing and planning skills were constantly exposed in groups. Bad planning and decisions compounded and accumulated, often leaving groups in total disarray. The situation was worsened by having the most impaired members chairing the meetings. Group Secretaries kept terrible minutes, often causing groups to have no idea what decisions they made in the past and keeping them unable to benefit from past experience. Such problems were magnified by the fact that the staff kept a much more accurate set of minutes, which patients were not allowed to borrow, and were therefore unerringly able to point out all the group's mistakes and misjudgments.

All of the previously mentioned group techniques can often arouse confusion, and their frequent use kept confusion at a high level. As mentioned before, many groups were filled with "creative chaos." It was typical in group sessions for tension and frustration to mount and for group sentiment to swing wildly this way and that, with therapists being content to have the experience itself be the chief benefit of therapy, rather than feeling a need to solve specific problems or make specific decisions. Finally, although patients and groups wished the confusion could be replaced by simple answers, therapists often told groups that "Confusion is beautiful."

Into this atmosphere of confusion, therapists constantly pumped A.A. concepts and phrases. Patients often became confused during their days of therapy and then found clarity and reason at night in A.A. meetings. Concrete group actions offered the best clarity, and these tended to be ones that involved sacrificing for each other, caring for each other, and carrying out some of the A.A. ideas, such as putting "first things first," being "willing to go to any length," and "making direct amends."

SHOCK, SURPRISE, AND HUMOR

Shock, surprise, and humor can all briefly depotentiate resistance and make it possible for an individual or a group to be receptive to a therapeutic suggestion. Another benefit is that they can make the therapeutic process more enjoyable and memorable. A third benefit, which will be covered in the next section on arousing one emotion and switching to another, is the ability to arouse humor and quickly switch to any other emotion a patient might need to experience.

A number of techniques and group experiences that have already been described are filled with shock, surprise, and humor. Patients' being greeted by applause after singing in the lobby or parading in turbans to quack at the ducks are both shocking and hilarious. Seeing the therapist suddenly jump up and throw all the program improvement suggestions into the trash can is shocking. Having the grocery store manager's jaw drop as he witnesses a group of alcoholics on an amends mission pushing shopping carts through the store's doors is humorous.

Here is another example:

The Chairman of the group spoke in a nearly inaudible voice. Both patients and staff repeatedly had to ask him to speak up or to repeat what he had said. Finally, the therapist proposed that the group make him a megaphone, so that he could be heard. The group approved the motion overwhelmingly.

The next day, the Chairman sat at the table at the front of the room with a cardboard megaphone, approximately two feet long, decorated with little pink elephants on a field of purple construction paper. The patients were very proud of their creation and both patients and staff members had to stifle laughter throughout the meeting every time the Chairman spoke through his megaphone.

After a few days, the therapist became concerned that continued laughter and ridicule might become abusive to the Chairman, so he made a motion to remove the requirement to use the megaphone. The Chairman seemed relieved, but the next time he spoke, the same feeble little voice came out. Group members expressed their irritation, but seemed resigned to having a Chairman they could not hear.

Suddenly, the therapist had an inspiration. He announced to the group: "The group made a megaphone for the Chairman in hopes that having to use it would motivate him to speak more loudly. That didn't work. I now understand why it didn't work. He became dependent on the megaphone to make his voice louder and failed to learn how to speak more loudly without it. It is clear what must be done. He must have an experience that will teach him how to speak loudly. Therefore, I make a motion that the Chairman be required to speak through the megaphone again, only this time he is to speak through the wrong end of it." The group approved the motion.

The Chairman spent the next several days having to place his entire head into the large end of the megaphone so that he could speak out of the small end, with a parade of little pink elephants marching a spiral path around the megaphone visible all the while. The scene was both funny and a bit surrealistic. Finally, after several days, he was relieved of his ordeal and, from that point on, he spoke loudly and clearly.

Another example is the time the group was angry at one of its members and approved the therapist's "off the wall" motion to shoot him at sunrise:

Shortly after the motion carried, members of the group began to grasp the implications of its rash and impulsive decision. How could they actually shoot Bob? And, if they didn't do what they had committed themselves to do, what horrible sacrifice would they have to make in order to get out of it?

Although the therapist might ordinarily have "made 'em sweat," over this problem, he felt somewhat charitable and also saw a way to help the group become more tightly bonded and create an experience that would live on as a fun recovery memory. As the group's discussion became increasingly tense, he came to the rescue by pointing out that there was nothing in the motion about guns. "You could shoot someone with something other than a gun, you know," he pointed out. Members of the group looked pleadingly at him, hoping for just a little more information. "Well, for example, you could shoot someone with rubber bands."

The group rejoiced. They had been let off the hook. In their glee, they spent a great deal of time planning the "execution." Many of the details were kept secret, but two group members asked repeatedly to be sure of the time and place of the staff's morning meeting. The staff knew that the group was going to come up with something the next morning and waited in curious anticipation.

The group did not disappoint the staff. Just after the staff meeting began, several group members knocked on the door. When granted access, they excitedly rolled a gurney into the room. On top of the gurney lay Bob, looking up grinning from a plastic body bag the group had somehow managed to find. During the group meeting that took place a short time later, the patients took delight in giving a full report of the activities of the "firing squad" that had marched outside at dawn and "executed" Bob.

Other humorous touches were provided by colorful language and imagery. Therapists enjoyed caricaturing the symptoms of addiction as a way of teaching patients about the reality of the disease. For example, when a patient tried to make his Discharge Plan seem adequate by presenting it well, even though the content was poor, the therapist spoke of "silver-plated shit." He said: "It looks good on the outside, but it's still just plain old shit on the inside."

Another scatological analogy was what the therapist called "the cat-shit approach to problem solving." He invoked this analogy whenever patients tried to ignore or cover up obvious problems: "I remember a house I lived in once, where a cat came to visit a plot of dirt just outside my living room window. That piece of dirt stank to high heaven—even though the cat scratched some dirt on top of it. That's what alcoholics and addicts do—throw a little dirt on top of their problems. But the trouble is, they still stink!"

Humor often helped patients to deal with issues they were overly sensitive about. One of the most sensitive issues was homophobia—patients' fear of homosexuality—which was maximized by the proximity to one another with which all those men lived, the interruption of their sex lives by their confinement, and the experiences some of them had had in jails and prisons.

The presence of homophobia could be utilized therapeutically on occasion. For example, one group contained two men· who became very close and effectively insulated each other from treatment and supported each other's denial. The therapist separated them by making a motion, which the group passed, to require the two men to hold hands wherever they went. Very quickly they began avoiding each other, so as not to look as if there were any "hanky panky" going on between them.

The most outrageous and funny incidents related to homophobia involved fingernail polish:

The group was at the point of voting on a sacrifice, but there was very little left to sacrifice. As was typical with many groups, problem had compounded problem, resulting in a huge mess with more sacrifices than the group could effectively keep track of. Meanwhile, several group members had been making antihomosexual insults and jokes. The therapist felt that it was time to give them an experience that would help remove the prejudice and break the tension with humor. He saw the mess the group was in with sacrifices and offered a solution.

"I make a motion," the therapist began, "that all sacrifices be consolidated into one of my choosing and that the group approve it without knowing what it is in advance."

Some group members objected. They were afraid of being tricked into doing something extremely unpleasant. One patient said: "It'll be shaving our heads, won't it?"

The therapist replied: "No, it has nothing to do with shaving heads. It's completely and easily reversible. It involves no pain whatever. And I think many of you will actually like it." Warily, the group voted and the motion barely passed. The therapist announced: "The sacrifice is for all group members to wear fingernail polish for a week. I will provide the polish, which you will put on during the afternoon group." Many groans were heard during and after this announcement.

During lunch hour, the therapist went out and purchased two bottles of the brightest, gaudiest, cheapest pink nail polish he could find. He brought them back to the unit and affixed new labels to the bottles. That afternoon, he presented the polish to the group. The new labels, now visible for the first time, proclaimed the color as "Homosexual Pink."

None of the patients appeared to have had any experience in applying nail polish. As a consequence, their nails were uniformly messy. Polish graced skin as well as nails. Few waited for the polish to dry before touching things and they applied numerous new coats without removing old coats, so the polish was lumpy and bumpy. It was a hilarious sight to watch these men, some young, some old, some with hands shaking, passing little bottles of pink polish around the room and touching up their nails.

AROUSING ONE EMOTION AND SWITCHING TO ANOTHER

A major portion of the recovery experience from addiction is emotional, but this crucial element is sometimes overlooked because of the focus on cognitive and behavioral aspects of treatment. It is very desirable, if not essential, for therapists to arouse as many powerful emotions in their patients as possible in a nondrinking, nonusing environment, so that they can learn how to experience and tolerate emotional arousal.

Many of the group therapy techniques already described are effective at arousing anger, frustration, fear, guilt, and anxiety, among other emotions. Therapists using these techniques need to keep the emotional component of therapy in mind at all times, so that they can take advantage of as many opportunities as they can to arouse strong affect and help patients learn how to handle it.

In spite of the capability of many of the previously described techniques for igniting emotional fireworks, there are always some patients who persistently stay at a shallow affective level or who avoid certain emotions which are more difficult for them than others. For example, the most difficult feelings for many passive women seem to be anger and aggression, while the most difficult feelings for many "tough guy" men are shame, public displays of tenderness, and any emotions that involve crying.

It is possible to help these emotionally-blocked patients by arousing an emotion in them that they find easy to experience and then switching them unexpectedly to one they are less comfortable with and need to learn about. This approach is possible because emotional arousal seems to be fairly generic. In other words, arousal is arousal. Once any emotion is aroused, any other emotion can be more easily reached from that point than from an unaroused state.

Patients who would rather laugh than cry are very difficult to move from their baseline to sadness or hurt or other emotions usually accompanied by crying. However, a therapist with a good sense of humor might find it easy to get such patients laughing. Then, once they are aroused, the job of getting them to feel crying-related emotions is fairly easy: Just abruptly change the subject and talk with potent imagery about subjects one knows the patients are bound to feel sad, hurt, etc., about. Childhood experiences are particularly effective, especially those related to loneliness, rejection, abandonment, or abuse.

GUIDELINES FOR BUILDING A GROUP

This section contains a set of guidelines and pointers. The goal of presenting them is to distill out of the foregoing examples and methods a few lessons and principles that will be applicable to practically any setting where group approaches may be used.

GROUP, NOT INDIVIDUAL, ISSUES ARE THE FIRST PRIORITY

A group must be cohesive and united in order to work effectively. There is no point attempting to do any therapy in a group before the group starts becoming a cohesive unit. Therapists need to remember that the group is the source of therapy, and the group therapist is the facilitator, or supervisor, of the group-as-therapist. Therefore, group therapists should avoid giving in to the temptation to try to help individuals with their problems until after the group is organized, because doing so would subvert the effectiveness of the actual therapy-giver. Therapists who attempt to help individuals prior to this time risk seeing the group fall into a pattern in which the therapist is the only helper and the group is nothing more than a passive, ineffective audience; or seeing the group sabotage or undo whatever therapeutic gains the group therapist is able to achieve.

ESTABLISH PRINCIPLES EARLY

One of the best ways to build a cohesive group is to help the group establish principles, goals, and priorities. The group has to know where it is going and why. In addition, it must be the one to choose its goals and principles; imposing them from without only creates rebellion. However, a subtly directive, permissive hypnotic approach can be very helpful during the initial period, to ensure that the group selects goals and principles that will actually be therapeutic.

In actual practice, the most effective practice a therapist can engage in during the formation of a group is to ask incessantly: "What are we here for?" There will be resistance to answering this question, from two levels, operating in unison. Individuals, impatient to get helped, will want to avoid this question and get on with having their needs met as quickly as possible. The group, wanting to evade responsibility for helping its members and preferring to place the responsibility on the therapist's shoulders, will repeatedly present apparently urgent individual problems for the therapist to solve. The therapist must resist these pressures and persevere singlemindedly until the group has established its goals.

Some of the many important questions that every group needs to address in order to know where it is going and why are: (a) What is the group here for? (b) How does the group make decisions? And how will the group keep track of its decisions? (c) How (behaviorally) shall the group help its members? (d) How open shall group members be with personal information? (e) What kinds of contact are encouraged and/or prohibited outside of group sessions? (f) What action(s) will the group take if a member uses alcohol or drugs? (g) What does the group expect from mem-

bers about attending sessions consistently and arriving on time?
(h) How much can group members say about what goes on in
group sessions to people who were not there? (i) What does the
group expect of its members with regard to A.A. or other Twelve
Step group attendance? (j) What does someone have to do to
become a group member? (k) How should the group handle new
members (those admitted to the group after it has started)? (l)
Under what conditions does a member graduate from the group?
(m) How will the group know if a member is in trouble? What
signs should it look for? (n) What should the group do to help a
member who is in trouble? (o) How will the group deal with violations of these policies and rules?

Make Sure the Group Polices Itself

Some of the important questions listed above relate to the
issue of how the group polices itself. The questions are always
about what the *group* expects from its members, and how it
responds to various behaviors, such as rule violations or signs
of relapse. The rules must be the group's rules and the sanctions must be the group's sanctions. Making or allowing the
therapist to be the disciplinarian is a formula for failure. If the
therapist is the judge, every group session will threaten to
become a tribunal. Patients will take sides and argue cases
instead of dealing with their disease and the therapist will run
the risk of becoming ineffective as the result of drawing fire
either from factions of the group or from the entire group for
making unpopular decisions.

Be a Teacher

One of the most effective roles that a group therapist can
assume during the crucial building phase especially, and throughout the life of the group as well, is that of teacher of group dynam-

ics. Therapists should directly address the group's need to arrive at the important decisions listed above and help structure the group's quest for these decisions. They should explain the reasoning behind and the value of the principles involved. They should share their experiences in working with both effective and ineffective groups as a way of instructing the group about what works and what does not work. Eventually, when the group abandons its attempts to get the therapist to fix its members, the group will begin to use the therapist appropriately as a resource that can offer knowledge that will help the group run smoothly and productively.

DON'T WORK HARDER THAN THE GROUP

Who should be working harder on a patient's recovery—the patient or the therapist? The obvious answer is: the patient. If the therapist is working harder on the patient's recovery than the patient is, the patient probably does not want to recover enough to do what it takes to achieve the result. In addition, the patient is in a position to manipulate the therapist by putting the therapist on a reinforcement schedule. When the patient appears to be recovering, the therapist feels rewarded, and when the patient regresses or relapses, the therapist feels punished. The whole time, the patient may not really give a damn one way or the other, but merely be content to "jerk around" the therapist while pursuing unstated, subterranean goals. To prevent this situation, patients must be kept from depending on their therapists to do their work for them.

This principle remains essentially unchanged in the transfer from individual to group dynamics. The therapist must not "do it for" the group either. If therapists find themselves becoming exhausted and notice that their groups are hardly budging, it is time for a new regime. The therapists need to let their groups know that they are unwilling to work harder than the groups do. They must be alert to those times when groups slack off or when they appeal to therapists to rescue or fix them, and respond by "just saying no."

Groups often refuse to take a direct "no" for an answer, and persist by using more indirect methods. They can be very clever and conspiratorial at these efforts, pursuing their goal by constantly asking questions, seeking guidance, acting helpless, and creating crises for their therapists to solve. To avoid falling prey to these games, therapists can use counter-games such as the following.

One method is to ask questions consistently instead of giving answers or directives (backward communication). Another is to flip-flop and equally support both sides of issues under discussion, so that groups will be forced make up their own minds. Another is to answer questions with vague generalities or cite principles without pointing out how to apply them. Another is to repeat a question or a request for guidance with a remark such as: "Yes, I wonder *how* the group is going to solve this problem." Another is for therapists to give obviously wrong or goofy answers to demonstrate that they cannot reliably be counted on to solve a group's problems for it. Eventually, groups give up when they realize that it is going to take more effort to get their therapists to do their work for them than it will to simply do it themselves.

MAKE THE GROUP RESPONSIBLE

This principle is closely allied with the previous one. When groups takes full responsibility for their personal recoveries, they will naturally work harder than their therapists on them. They will be active participants instead of passive recipients of services. To encourage this state of affairs, therapists must make clear to their groups that the groups alone are responsible for the consequences of their decisions and actions.

They should communicate that they have no qualms about allowing individuals or groups to experience these consequences fully, whether they are positive and enjoyable or severe and painful. They must overcome all urges to step in and rescue groups

from bad decisions, but do everything possible to help the groups
learn from these experiences.

Welcome, Encourage, and Utilize Resistance

Resistance is not a bad thing. It is not a problem. It is merely
a signal that a different therapeutic approach is needed.
Therapists need to be like good salespersons, who welcome the
challenge of objections from their prospects. Many sales techniques are built completely upon the process of overcoming objections and will not work at all unless a prospect resists. Therefore,
many salespersons eagerly anticipate and thrive on resistance. By
using Erickson-inspired techniques, therapists can similarly thrive
on the resistance of their groups.

Plan Ahead

Sometimes it is effective to let a group run itself. But a steady
diet of self-direction can give free rein to the sickness of addiction.
Remember that groups of addicted people are full of addicts. Left
unguided, they are bound to regress and begin allowing denial,
impaired judgment, dishonesty, and other symptoms to flourish;
and group-sanctioned drinking and drug use will not be far
behind. Therapists need to keep groups on track and the best way
to do that is to plan ahead strategically.

Letting whatever comes up first determine which subject the
group will focus on for the rest of the session is not a particularly
effective way to work. Although the addicts who make up the
group might be working hard on recovery, they are just as likely,
if not more likely, to be filled with anxiety or denial or some other
irrational process that has more to do with determining what subject comes up at that moment than actual clinical need. It is pref-
erable for therapists to decide in advance what the group ought
to focus on and begin the group in a way that ensures that the

group will address that issue. In other words, therapists should "set up" their groups often. Of course, therapists should be flexible, since issues they may not have been aware of beforehand can often surface during the session. It is better to have to abandon a plan occasionally than to habitually operate without one.

BE PREPARED TO SWITCH GEARS OFTEN

Groups never stay the same; therefore, group therapists can never stay the same. Groups are organic, evolving, changing things. At any given stage or mode of functioning, a group may need a completely different kind of therapy from the one needed at the stage just before it, and another completely different kind of therapy at the next stage. Therapists need to be able to switch quickly and completely from one appropriate mode of therapy to another. With practice, they will often be able to anticipate what is likely to be needed next. However, groups frequently surprise even the most experienced therapists, so they also need to be able to react quickly to changing conditions.

For example, a therapist with a new group that starts out with three members and stays at that level for a month may get used to having only three patients and is likely to spend a lot of time on individual members of the group and their problems, almost like having a shared three-way individual therapy session. This kind of process at this stage of a group's development is fine, since there is time for it and there is not much of a group available for a more group-focused process.

But what happens in this example when six more members are added to the group in one week and the size swells from three to nine? If the therapist tries to keep the same process going, no one will be happy. Older members will feel cheated out of the attention they used to feel was lavished on them. They will resent the new members. New members will be confused, sensing and reacting to the lingering feelings. Factions may form. The group may not find its own identity or reason for being. The therapist needs to quickly abandon the old process, switch to a new one, and help all members, old and new, to adjust to and accept the new way of doing things.

PAY ATTENTION TO MULTIPLE LEVELS

This is just a reminder to therapists to pay attention to both individual psychodynamics and group dynamics. Although with groups the group process is the top priority, individual issues cannot be ignored, since it is the purpose of group therapy to influence individual behavior. On the other hand, therapists who ignore the group process in their zeal to effect individual changes will sooner or later become mired in unhealthy processes that make their goal impossible to achieve. Make a habit of "tuning in" to both levels often and repeatedly. Eventually, it becomes possible to be continuously aware of both levels simultaneously.

LOOK OUT FOR UNHEALTHY GROUP PROCESSES

Therapists should keep their eyes open for patterns that groups often fall into which can diminish or cripple their therapeutic effectiveness (such as Bion's "basic assumption groups," as described by Rioch, 1970).

By far the worst offender is *individual therapy with group audience*. In this pattern, individuals present their problems one at a time and the therapist provides individual therapy for each one as the group looks on. The problem with this pattern is that it is inefficient and, from a group process point of view, an avoidant rather than a working pattern. It is inefficient, because patients can never get enough good individual therapy this way, yet they get no group therapy. It is avoidant, because it allows all members except the one designated "it" to avoid therapy. Often, things going on at the group level that go unnoticed because of the focus on individual dynamics have a lot to do with who gets chosen for the individual work. That is, there is often collusion which results in one person "taking the fall" for the rest of the group.

Individual therapy with group audience typically begins when a therapist starts a group by asking if there are any issues. Not only is this a lazy way to run a group, because it requires no planning and little imagination, but it is asking for trouble because individuals are bound to respond to the request for issues by bringing up individual ones. Any therapists found allowing this kind of process to go on in their groups for session after session should be rushed immediately to their nearest group dynamics seminar.

The other most serious type of group process is actually a category of different subtypes: *codependent groups*. A codependent group is like a codependent person. It enables the symptoms of addiction to progress by encouraging them, covering them up, or acting like they are not happening when they are. Therapists need to work extra hard at becoming aware of the times when groups slip into codependent processes, for several reasons. First, codependent group processes are subtle and often difficult to distinguish from processes that are actually helping. Second, they are comfortable. When groups are in a codependent process, most patients feels good, interactions are often calm, and therapists often feel well-liked, well-praised, and successful.

Beware! All is not well when all seems well. These are terminally ill, extremely impaired and pain-filled individuals. Groups filled with such patients logically cannot be calm and happy. There should be plenty of turmoil, clashing egos, anxiety, guilt, rage, shame, shouting, and tears. This is not to say that all sessions should be dramatic and "gut-wrenching," since keeping high drama going can also be a form of codependent process. It is important to have steady injections of reality: real problems, real feelings, and real pain. Codependent groups create and believe in unreality. Working, productive groups deal with reality.

One pattern of codependent group is that of *rescuing and fixing* individual members. Helping members is one thing. It involves offering support while the members go through the agony of recovery and struggle with their problems. Rescuing and fixing consists of rescuing members from the pain and fixing the member's problems for them. This pattern makes members happy, because they either feel worthwhile as the result of doing something for someone else or they enjoy being the recipient of gifts. The only problem is that the rescuing and fixing keeps everyone sick. Therapists need to monitor groups constantly for even the slightest tendency to rescue members from pain instead of supporting them as they go through pain. They should also frequently teach their groups the difference between these behaviors; establish principles which, when accepted, prevent rescuing; and confront rescuing behaviors whenever they arise.

Another codependent pattern is *pairing off*. This pattern occurs when pairs of members become so close and so deeply involved with each other that they effectively shield each other from the therapy. Within their dyad, they often do the most blatant and damaging codependent things. This pattern often develops in the group, in full view of the therapist. However, it also develops in secret, with the pairing occurring at times and in places of which the therapist has no knowledge. Sometimes, only one dyad forms, but at other times, everyone pairs off.

Another codependent group process is *secret-keeping*. When this pattern occurs, the entire group colludes to keep some item or items of information away from the therapist. For example, if a sick dyad forms outside of the group and other group members know about it, they may keep the therapist from knowing about it. Secret-keeping is destructive in itself and it compounds other destructive processes by keeping them from being confronted and resolved.

Another codependent process is *all talk and no action*. Groups often perform for the benefit of their therapists by putting on a show of loving concern or commitment that ends when the session ends. When it comes down to attending A.A. meetings, contacting each other between sessions, or becoming productively involved in each other's lives in more than a superficial way, such groups prove that they are much longer on talk than they are on action. They are answering the question: "How far are you willing to go for your recovery?" by their actions, indicating that they are not willing to go very far at all.

Another codependent group process is *punishing instead of loving*. This process occurs when the group is more interested in maintaining order than in pursuing recovery and attempts to achieve order by punishing those who misbehave. This method of discipline is ineffective, because it creates resentment and it definitely undermines recovery. But it makes sense that groups of addicts would select it, given the history of angry, physical punishment that so many patients received as children and then continued to receive as adults.

The self-esteem of most addicted patients is battered; they need love, not punishment. However, they find it difficult both to give and to accept love. Therapists should make it a top priority to help create an atmosphere of genuine caring and love within groups by leading them to perform deeds that convey love in ways that patients cannot deny, thereby enabling them to learn to accept love. Thus, all members learn how to give love by participating in loving acts. Loving behavior need not be all tender and sweet; it can be tough, too. Sacrifices are a form of tough love and so is saying no to unreasonable demands, expecting responsibility, and allowing group members' addiction-related consequences to engulf them.

A final negative group process is the *tendency to create family roles*, such as hero, scapegoat, and the rest. It is very common for patients to fall into old family roles as they become involved in groups. This tendency is especially pronounced when ages and sexes of members remind other members of their family members. For example, older men often become younger men's and women's fathers, and older women become mothers. When most members are older, the younger members either become difficult, rebellious children or scapegoats, or they become perfect, able-to-do-no-wrong heroes. These projections become particularly vivid and distressing if one or more group members experience others as resembling people from the past who seriously abused them.

Therapists can help individual group members understand themselves and their disease by properly interpreting such projections and helping individuals learn both how to recognize what is behind their irrational reactions and how to react more rationally and adaptively. At the group level, they need to stop groups from becoming alcoholic or addicted families. All those families did before was churn out new addicts. What is needed is a new, healthy family, and a well functioning group can be just that.

5

Influencing Family Process

Families are profoundly affected by chemical dependency. The two most notable effects are the development of codependency in individual family members and the changes that take place in the overall family system.

CODEPENDENCY AS ADDICTION TO
AN ADDICTED PERSON

One way to understand codependency is to view it as a separate addictive disease in which the "substance" to which a person is addicted is a person or relationship (or a type of person or relationship or relationship experience) rather than a chemical.

Support for this view comes from work by Richard Solomon (Solomon, 1980; Solomon & Corbit, 1974), in which he posits that hedonic arousal of an organism (pleasure or pain) can, with repetition of a stimulus or class of stimuli, lead to a buildup of arousal by the organism that opposes the original stimulus. This "opponent process," when added to or overlaid upon the organism's initial reaction to the stimulus, can create dynamics typical of addiction.

For example, according to Solomon's theory, a person who

repeats an extremely pleasurable activity over and over will gradually, with each repetition, build up in the nervous system an opponent reaction consisting of pain. This phenomenon is not unlike a color afterimage, in which a person's nervous system builds up an experience of green in reaction to staring for a long period at a red stimulus. The onset of the pain lags just a bit after the onset of the pleasure and lasts somewhat past the end of the pleasure. The more times the activity is repeated, the longer the pain lasts after stopping. The person begins to notice that the pleasurable activity does not feel as strong as it once did and that terrible feelings come when the activity stops.

In short, the person experiences tolerance and withdrawal, which are the hallmarks of addiction. The new and unique contribution of this theory is the suggestion that addiction (or, more conservatively, addiction-like phenomena) can be associated with *any* pleasurable (or any painful) activity, whether the pleasure is the result of drug use, eating, gambling, or anything—even falling in love.

There is an interesting and important side note about Solomon's theory: the concept of "savings." According to the theory (supported by numerous human and animal studies), an opponent process once built up is never the same again. It may appear to die out if the stimulation that led to its existence is stopped. However, if the stimulation is resumed, the opponent process reaches its previous maximum strength in a much shorter time than it took to reach that strength initially. In other words, once someone has developed an addiction, he or she will always have that addiction.

One of the most common addictions is what some people call "love." Addictive love is exciting and heady. Love addicts *fall* in love *madly*. They become *crazy* about someone and try to make that person theirs. Love addicts treat their lover like a substance and become compulsively preoccupied with getting, maintaining, and using a supply of him or her. After awhile, being with the object of their affection no longer feels as good as it did in the beginning, but if they try to end the relationship, they find that they cannot stay away. They have begun to experience tolerance and withdrawal. Love addiction can create extremely dysfunctional relationships and is a powerful contributor to phenomena such as domestic violence and divorce.

Addiction to love is bad enough, but even worse is addiction to love with a chemically dependent person. This condition is what is meant here by codependency. A codependent person is obsessed with and dependent on a chemically dependent person, who is obsessed with and dependent on alcohol and drugs. Codependent people often complain about the addicted person's addiction, but they also "enable" the addiction by supplying the necessary chemicals, rescuing and protecting the addicted person when he or she gets into trouble, and engaging in other behaviors that keep the addiction going. Often, they have a vested interest in keeping the addiction going, so that the addicted person will be disabled and therefore need them, thus ensuring their continued supply of the addicted person's time and attention.

The Altered Family System

A family may be viewed as a homeostatic system whose component parts are the roles that family members occupy. Wegscheider (1981) provides an excellent description of chemically dependent family roles. Family systems become accustomed to having one or more chemically dependent members and the roles appear as if they had been built to accommodate those members. Some families get that way by a gradual process of adaptation to the changes in the chemically dependent member as his or her disease progresses. Other families arise pre-built to accommodate a chemically dependent member, because they were formed by the marriage of two people who were a part of the same kind of system during their childhood. Once a family system has accommodated to chemical dependency, the roles are set and the system works very hard to make sure that every member stays in role. In this way, a family's ordinarily adaptive tendency to seek a homeostatic balance serves only to perpetuate a deadly problem.

If a chemically dependent—or codependent—person is to recover, he or she must make some very drastic changes. In order to make those necessary changes, the recovering person risks violating family role definitions and receiving the sanctions that the family system administers as part of its role-policing function. Since these sanctions can be very punishing, many who would otherwise recover give in to the pressure and abandon all recovery efforts.

THE NEED FOR FAMILY INVOLVEMENT IN TREATMENT

It is clear that both codependent individuals and family systems contribute to the problem of chemical dependency by encouraging the chemically dependent person's symptoms of addiction and obstructing change. In fact, they so strongly perpetuate the problem that it is difficult to imagine how treatment could be effective if it ignored them. With this observation as a backdrop, the remainder of the chapter is devoted to treatment methods.

Techniques presented in this chapter are mainly descriptions of how previously presented group therapy techniques can be applied to the family, which is, after all, a special type of group. This chapter is, then, less about family process per se than it is about group techniques, and more specifically about techniques that needed to be developed to help deal with a unique type of multiple-family group treatment situation.

DESCRIPTION AND GOALS OF FAMILY THERAPY

Hospital inpatients and their families attended multiple-family groups once a week. Outpatients and their families attended similar multiple-family groups. Family members only (without addicted patients attending) could attend a special group that was offered daily.

The therapy contained a strong didactic element, in which therapists taught families that everyone in an addicted family was sick from the disease of addiction. As part of their nonsubstance addiction, they were told, family members suffered in every category of their lives—physically, psychologically, socially, interpersonally, and vocationally—and could eventually die of their disease. In spite of the negative consequences, they continued to behave in ways that perpetuated the disease, and they were unable to recognize how maladaptive their behavior was. In other words, family members and significant others of chemically addicted persons also suffered from denial and delusion.

GOALS

Therapists pursued two kinds of goals: *Outcome goals*, or desired behavioral outcomes for the patients and families; and *Process goals*, or objectives whose attainment helped therapists to manage the therapy situation (Lovern & Zohn, 1982).

Outcome goals were related to the following important needs of chemically dependent patients and their families: The family members needed to discover that they had problems in addition to those caused by the chemically dependent person's behavior, and that help was available for them. In addition, both chemically dependent and nonchemically dependent family members needed to feel mutually understood and to begin to cooperate more effectively. Third, since both chemically addicted and nonaddicted family members had failed at previous attempts to stop the progression of addiction, neither was likely to expect the therapy to help them. Therapy therefore needed to provide an experience so convincingly powerful that all participants could dare to believe that it could be effective.

Based on these needs, outcome goals were: (a) cessation of denial by nonchemically addicted family members and acceptance of and participation in a recovery program such as Al-Anon or Alateen; (b) mutual understanding and cooperation in their respective recovery efforts by both chemically addicted and non-chemically addicted family members; and (c) the experiencing of a powerful emotional event by family members to build the expectancy that the therapy is potent enough to help patients change their lives.

Process goals were related to the conditions and limitations of the treatment setting: Family therapists were confronted with a unique and challenging situation. On any given week, as many as 30 chemically dependent inpatients were represented by up to 40 or 50 family members, resulting in groups as large as 70 or 80 members (with 50 or 60 being average).

With so many patients, it was difficult for therapists to ensure that every participant would pay attention and feel involved in the therapeutic process. Most meetings contained a few new participants who were fearful about taking part or who defiantly refused to listen or participate. In addition, some participants tried to challenge the therapist or undermine the therapy by diverting it into a nontherapeutic direction. For example, family members who were chemically addicted and denying that fact occasionally attended meetings drunk or high and created disturbances, while others tried to start debates or other long-winded digressions, so that the therapy might be reduced to useless interactions ranging from intellectual discussions to shouting matches. There was an ever-present potential for the groups to degenerate into unruly crowds.

Since therapists could easily be overwhelmed by this kind of situation, lose control of the group, and wind up watching helplessly as the therapy session became a useless or even destructive event, they needed to stay a step or more ahead of the group, to involve participants actively, attentively, and cooperatively, and to lead the group in a productive direction.

Given this situation, process goals were for therapists to: (a) lead the group and avoid being led by it; (b) create open-minded responsiveness in as many participants as possible; and (c) utilize

the characteristics and productions of all participants to orches-
trate an experience for them that would be therapeutic in spite
of all obstacles.

Overall Treatment Approach

Therapists evolved a format that was tailored to the situation
and permitted them to accomplish therapy in the large and drastically changing groups they faced each week. Practically every session began with a didactic lecture covering some aspect of the
family disease of addiction. The lectures were designed not only
to present facts but also to "set up" the group for the therapy that
followed: Each week, therapists established ground rules and principles, bound all participants to commitments to participate fully,
and ensured that recovery-related topics were discussed in ways
that would promote recovery.

In the early days of the program, groups were small and resembled more traditional multiple-family groups. All participants sat
in a circle in a large room and most of them had a chance to share
thoughts and feelings spontaneously. Later, the size and composition of the groups reached the point where traditional methods
became inoperative. As the group grew, the simple circle became
first a series of concentric circles, and then formed into an "audience" configuration, with curved, semicircular rows facing the
"stage" where the therapist or therapists sat.

Usually, the team of therapists accepted this configuration and
sat in the chairs the group left for them, but sometimes they con-
founded it by sitting elsewhere, by spreading out and sitting in
different locations throughout the room, or by roaming from location to location. Therapists created these variations in order to
break the groups' expectations, so that they could be influenced
more pliably. During one session, the first of two therapists sat in
the "reserved" therapist chair, and the second therapist unexpectedly popped up here and there in different parts of the group,
dramatically asking questions or making comments about the first

therapist's lecture or about the behavior and responses of the group. In another session, therapist one and therapist two essentially induced hypnosis in each other by indirect suggestions as the members of the group looked on and found the contagion of trance spreading to them as well.

BASIC APPROACH AND VARIATIONS

The first example is a description of a "model" multiple-family group, which shows a core method that can be improvised from or elaborated on as called for by variations in the needs, dynamics, mood, attitude (and other variables) of the individual patients and individual families involved and of the greater group. Additional examples are descriptions of modifications of this basic method.

A Model Group

Unconscious conditioning. What a therapist does at the very beginning of a group can set the emotional tone and establish implicit rules for the participants' conduct for the rest of the meeting. The therapist in this case expects the large group to be unruly and wants it to learn from the start that it is to pay close attention and respond to his behavior, even—or especially—subtle and nonverbal behavior.

> The therapist strode into the room alone, just a minute or two before the scheduled starting time, and sat in the chair around which the group was arranged in concentric half circles. He carried a clipboard, and, after seating himself, looked carefully at the papers on it, then up at the group, then back at the papers. He aroused curiosity in those who watched or were aware of his behavior by seeming to be comparing individuals or families in the group with items on his papers and nodding silently to himself as if each person or

family he noted fitted into some plan he had in mind. Finally, he looked back at his watch and noticed that it was exactly the group's starting time.

During these few moments, some members of the group silently watched the therapist and waited, but many, especially newcomers, carried on loud conversations the way groups or audiences often do while waiting for a show or event to begin. But the event had already begun. As the therapist noticed the time, he sat erect and looked sternly at the group. He did nothing more, just looked. When the hum of conversation did not lower, he scowled. When it rose, he looked disgusted and shifted in his seat. When it lowered, he leaned forward and looked expectantly alert. When it rose, he fidgeted impatiently, tapping his pen on the clipboard. When it lowered again, he leaned forward once again with expectant alertness.

The therapist paired his nonverbal expressions of disapproval and impatience with increases in the volume of sound coming from the group, and posture and expression of readiness with decreases in volume, until the group became more and more quiet. Finally, the group became eerily, stonily quiet. The therapist continued to just look, keeping the group quiet with his gaze. When conversation erupted once again, the therapist looked extremely disgusted and even more impatient. The group quieted down again. The therapist just looked again. Finally, after a number of repetitions, the group stayed quiet. As the therapist watched and waited, a certain level of discomfort arose in the group. This tension mounted further as the therapist continued to watch and wait. Finally, he relieved the discomfort by asking: "Is everyone ready?"

By pairing his nonverbal behaviors with specific group behaviors, the therapist was engaging in *unconscious conditioning* (Erickson & Rossi, 1979). What he conditioned the group to do by this technique was twofold. First, he conditioned the group to be silent so that the meeting could begin. But there had to be an additional goal, since this approach would have been a bit heavy-handed and time-consuming if the therapist's only goal had been to achieve silence. The second, more important, goal was to teach the group to pay close attention to the therapist at a nonverbal as well as verbal level, to wait to do anything until told or allowed by him to do so, and to follow his directions without having to be told what they were.

Shock, confusion-restructuring, and therapeutic binds. The next step the therapist took toward making this unwieldy group manage-able was to depotentiate participants' resistant mental sets with psychological shock, modify their expectancies with the confusion-restructuring approach, and consolidate their commitment to par-ticipate by presenting them with a therapeutic bind (Erickson & Rossi, 1979).

Once silence was achieved, the therapist began a lecture about alcohol and drug dependency. He delivered it in an earnest, tough, emotional tone, filled it with frightening facts, and illustrated it with vivid visual imagery. The combination was carefully designed to be as shocking and emotionally arousing as possible.

> The therapist's face seemed angry or indignant, and his voice rose until it was louder than seemed appropriate. Participants were taken aback by him, uncertain what to make of him. His first sentence was a question that also sounded like a challenge. He asked the group if anyone had any idea how many people had died from a certain disease that at that time was receiving a great deal of attention in the press. Some members guessed and the group quickly arrived at a consensus that the deaths numbered 50 or so. The ther-apist reminded the group of the urgency of public health warnings about this disease and the amount of fear sur-rounding it. Heads nodded.
>
> Then the therapist asked the group to guess the death rate associated with alcohol use. Several inaccurate guesses fol-

lowed, after which the therapist announced that the correct
figure was 205,000 per year. (United States Department of
Health, Education, and Welfare, 1974). "Two hundred and
five thousand deaths per year," the therapist repeated and
then paused. "That's a lot of deaths. A lot more than 50," he
said and paused again. "I sat down and figured out how
often someone dies an alcohol-related death: Once every two
and a half minutes. That means that, while we sit here in this
room tonight, 36 American lives will be lost to alcohol.
Thirty-six! And that doesn't include all the deaths caused by
other drugs or even tobacco."

The therapist continued the lecture, comparing the
alcohol-related death rate to the lives lost in the Vietnam war,
observing that, over the same 10 year period, assuming the
same rate, alcohol killed over 35 times as many people as war.
"Thirty-five times more deadly than war! Think of it! I think
we have a war going on right now. A silent war, but a deadly
war. Or maybe it's more like a plague. Maybe it's our modern
day version of the black plague."

Next, he began to summon some vivid visual images to
bring home the impact of that high number of deaths in a
way that the group could palpably experience. He brought
up the mass suicides of the cult followers of Jim Jones in the
jungle of Guyana. "Do you remember the difficulties they
had disposing of those bodies? The heat caused them to
decompose quickly, and some of them just exploded. There
were so many that the authorities didn't know what to do with
them. And there were just 900. What would you do with
205,000 bodies? Can you imagine how high a *pile* that would
make? Huh? What if you stacked them like cordwood in a
good sized stadium? How full would it get? How would you
feel being there, looking at those bodies?"

He encouraged the group to mentally experience as many
details as possible of such a scene, in as many sensory modalities as possible: sight, smell, touch, etc. The order, pacing,
and dramatic manner with which he presented his lecture,

with each vivid image being more horrible than the last, with his voice tone and volume rising and falling, and with his facial expression and body gestures adding emphasis, combined cumulatively to shock the audience, disorient their resistant mental sets, and unsettle whatever expectancies they had brought with them to the therapy situation.

With the group temporarily disoriented by this dramatic display, the therapist applied the *confusion-restructuring* approach and began to offer some suggestions to help participants structure their experiences. He told them that the problem was serious and required a serious response on their parts. "Do you see how bad this problem is? How powerful? If you're going to even begin to make a dent in it, you've got to be completely committed. You've got to be willing to go to any length whatever. You've got to do whatever it takes."

He continued: "One thing you've got to realize is what your role is here tonight. Some of you no doubt think you're just here to help *him* get well, to 'provide support.' Well, you'd better think again. You're all patients here. You're all affected by this terrible disease and it could kill every one of you, whether you're the one who drinks or uses drugs or not.

"Another thing you've got to do is be *completely honest*, holding back *nothing*. This disease thrives in the dark. If you hide anything about it, anything at all, that gives it license to grow and grow and grow. It's like having all but a little piece of a tumor removed. Whatever part of it you keep secret, that's the part that will kill you. You've got to be completely honest even if it's personal or embarrassing. We're fighting for life here, not trying to look good or run a popularity contest."

In essence, the therapist told the participants that they would have to make the following commitments: (a) to resolve sincerely to do whatever would be necessary to fight alcohol and drug addiction; (b) to accept the role of patient instead of observer, helper, or supporter; and (c) to agree to be absolutely honest about any subject, no matter how personal or private. He painted a picture of these commitments that was quite extreme; in fact, too extreme for any of the participants to be realistically willing to agree to them 100 percent. However, if they agreed to only 50 percent of these commitments, that level of cooperation would be adequate for the therapist's purposes. There was thus room for resistance. The therapist was employing the *providing-a-worse-alternative* technique, that is, demanding an extreme behavior and settling for a less extreme behavior that is a member of the same category.

Finally, the therapist introduced a bind as a way of sealing the agreement of all participants to behave in the manner suggested. He announced, in a slow, deliberate, and impressive tone: "This is what is expected of you, and *nothing less. (Pause)* If you won't go along with these conditions, *I want you to GET . . . OUT . . . N-O-O-OW!*" Then, he waited. And he waited some more. And, when it seemed as if he had waited more than an adequate length of time, he waited a bit longer. As he waited, he scanned the group, looking deeply into the eyes of each participant while wearing a fiery, fierce expression and leaning forward in his chair as if he were about to jump out of it at any instant.

The air was tense and highly charged. No one moved; participants seemed frozen in their seats. Absolute silence prevailed. Some participants' faces were frozen and blank. Others looked down at their laps or their feet. Finally, the therapist broke the silence, but not in a way that provided any relief from the tension. He continued his intense glare and asked: "Well? Who's leaving? I want you to think about it. Because, if you stay, you're committed to all those things I said. Each and every one of them. Willing to go to *any* length. *All* of you patients. *Completely* honest, no matter what. Come on. Who's leaving? You heard me. If you don't like it, *get out.*" He paused again for another uncomfortably long time. Still no one budged.

The bind was a presentation of two choices: either to do nothing or to get up and leave. It was much easier to do noth-

ing than to get up in the middle of the meeting and make
a spectacle of oneself, especially in light of the preceding lecture. Anyone who dared to leave would be admitting that he
was on the side of addiction and did not care for the lives of
the others in the room. However, choosing to do nothing,
while easier at that moment, carried with it a serious and far-
ranging commitment. In this situation, all participants chose
the easier-now-more-difficult-later option over the more-
difficult-now-easier-later one. Along with the bind, the therapist provided a strong challenge, which is similar to the
challenges hypnotists make when, for example, they suggest
that a subject's arm will be rigid, then say: "*Try* to bend it."

What if someone had actually gotten up and left? The therapist had to be ready for this possibility and he was. He was
quite prepared to accept or even welcome anyone's leaving,
because that would only increase the drama of the situation
and double the commitment of those who stayed. He could
comment to the remaining participants afterward that not
everyone cares enough or is courageous enough to make a
strong commitment like they had, thereby strongly positively
reinforcing their choice and adding even more to their
commitment.

At this point, the group is "primed" for therapy. Before the session began, participants were a diverse assortment of people, some
of whom were inpatients and the rest of whom had in common,
as far as they knew, only the fact that they were related to the inpatients. There were many of them, they had no unified group purpose or identity, and their motivation to take part in a therapeutic
process was questionable at best. Now they were all conditioned
to following the therapist's directions, even nonverbal ones; and
they were committed to adopting the role of patient, going to
whatever length was necessary and being completely honest. On
top of all that, they were aroused emotionally and therefore likely
to be ready at any point to "let it all hang out."

The therapist next selected an issue for discussion by this

"primed" group, taking care that the issue would be relevant to participants' needs. Which issue he selected depended on a number of factors, such as the composition of the group and what the therapist knew was going on between the inpatients and their families. In this situation, the family members were almost all wives of the male inpatients, with only one or two other relationships represented (such as an adult daughter, who was also married, possibly to an alcoholic, and a brother). Several patients were trying to placate their wives or prevent divorces and it was apparent that a number of wives had been deeply hurt by the antics of their husbands, but were focusing on trying to solve all their problems by making these "bad boys" change and behave well, rather than admitting that they had problems of their own that were not dependent for solution on whether their husbands changed.

Backward communication. The therapist selected the issue of how similar the emotional symptoms of chemical dependency are for both addicted persons and their nonaddicted spouses. This topic would occupy the group interaction phase of the group session, now that the introductory phases were over:

The therapist finally broke the long pause by commenting: "I guess we're ready to get started. I think what we need to do tonight is discuss what it's like to be married to an alcoholic or an addict. Is anyone here married to an alcoholic or addict?" As hands rose, he looked around the room, noted each wife, and checked his clipboard to verify the information there. "I see," he said, and then, he looked up at the air just above the center of the group and asked: "What's it like for *you*, uh . . . ," then looking directly at her, "Mrs. Smith?"
      "Well," she replied nervously, "I guess it's been tough."
      "I'll bet it's been *very* tough," the therapist affirmed. "What's an example of how tough it's been?"

The therapist continued the questioning, employing the *backward communication* technique (Lovern, 1980), which is described in the previous chapter. As he asked questions of one wife after another, they responded by relating stories of literal horrors. One wife told of a hiding place she had built in her bedroom closet, where she could place herself behind a barrel and see by the reflection in a mirror turned at the proper angle whether her husband was drunk or if he was likely to be violent. Another wife told of several different times she had sat in terror with her husband holding a gun to her head all night, insulting and threatening her and accusing her of having an affair with a neighbor whom she did not even know. The therapist reinforced each wife who told an honest story and used her example to encourage others to follow suit.

Common everyday trance and spontaneous regression. Common everyday trances are "those momentary pauses when the . . . person is quietly looking off into the distance or staring at something, as he or she apparently reflects inward" (Erickson & Rossi, 1979). Participants could frequently be observed sitting quietly and unblinkingly with their gazes fixed on nothing in particular; nodding slowly in unconscious agreement; or becoming cataleptic for brief periods—especially while other participants were relating vivid and emotionally stirring stories. These were signs that participants were entering spontaneous trances and would doubtless be more responsive to suggestions. The therapist observed and made mental note of these occurrences to gauge who was being reached by the process and to decide how to time the delivery of therapeutic suggestions, so that the right participants could be given suggestions at their most responsive times.

Occasionally, as she listened, a participant developed a *spontaneous regression*, in which she partially regressed to or relived an event from her past that was similar to the experience being recounted by the participant to whom she was listening. Often, one participant having this kind of experience would trigger others, until the entire room was awash in emotion. It was not unusual for participants to hold one another up or clutch each other tightly to form a hugging and sobbing subgroup. The therapist had to take care to ensure that all participants were "back" by the end of this kind of session.

As the wives continued to tell their stories, the therapist extracted from them a list of emotional symptoms, with which all participants agreed. He asked a nonwife member of the group to draw a vertical line down the middle of the blackboard across the room and write these items on one side. Soon the list, which invariably contained the same or similar items each time this topic was discussed with a family group, was complete. It contained: (a) fear, worry, dread, and helplessness; (b) guilt and shame; (c) anger and resentment; (d) low self-esteem, depression, and self-pity; (e) dishonesty and denial; and (f) a feeling of not being able to live *with* and not being able to live *without* the chemically dependent spouse.

When the list was complete, the therapist read it back to the group to ensure that it accurately represented their emotional symptoms. He made a point of using the term "emotional *symptoms*" repeatedly to underscore the idea that nonaddicted family participants had a disease. The therapist often labeled participants' experiences, or restated what they said, in new words that carried implications they may have been unaware of, but which the therapist felt would help them see their situations in ways that gave them new options or solutions. They accepted both the list and the terminology.

Next, the therapist changed the subject:

> "O.K., now we've listed the emotional symptoms of living with an alcoholic or addict, and everybody agrees on the list. Now, let's talk about the emotional symptoms of *being* an alcoholic or addict." Then, he began the backward communication process with the alcoholics and addicts in the room: "Fred, what's it like for you? What emotional symptoms do you have?"

The backward communication process continued, with Fred answering, the therapist accepting his answer and modifying it, then asking Mike, Mike answering, etc., until the group had come up with a list of the emotional symptoms of being chemically dependent. The final list, which another volunteer wrote on the blackboard next to the first list, was: (a) fear, worry, dread, and helplessness; (b) guilt and shame; (c) anger and resentment; (d) low self-esteem, depression, and self-pity; (e) dishonesty and denial; and (f) a feeling of not being able to live *with* and not being able to live *without* alcohol or drugs. In other words, the lists were identical, with the exception that the addicted patients felt that they couldn't live with or without drugs or alcohol, and the nonaddicted wives felt that way about their addicted husbands. After the lists were up on the board and the group had noted their similarity, the therapist commented:

"You see, the emotional symptoms are the same. But the emotional symptoms aren't the only ones that are the same. There are physical symptoms too. How many here have headaches?" Hands rose, and it was obvious that both addicted and nonaddicted participants had headaches. The therapist asked another question: "How many of you have stomach or intestinal trouble, including ulcers?" Again, the hands rose, and again there were equal proportions of addicted and nonaddicted persons among those with symptoms. "I want you to know that I didn't plant people here or check in advance to see how many of you had these problems. This is just how it is. The symptoms are the same, both emotional and physical."

The therapist did not stop there. He brought up another kind of symptom. "Now I want to ask the wives to think of how it felt breaking up a relationship with someone, or how it feels being home alone with your alcoholic or addict being in the hospital. How about it? Do any of you get restless? You know: When you're standing up, you want to sit down, and when you're sitting down, you want to stand up. Or maybe you want to jump out of your skin entirely."

Mrs. Jones admitted that she had been feeling restless about her husband's absence. Mrs. Brown mentioned that she got restless too, but something else bothered her more: the way her emotions kept changing, crying one minute and laughing the next. Another spouse talked about not being able to think about anything but her husband. As the wives continued to describe their experiences, the therapist constructed another list.

Then the therapist turned to query the inpatients: "What did it feel like for the addicts and alcoholics in the room to come off of chemicals? What was alcohol and drug withdrawal like?" One by one the patients described their symptoms, which turned out to include restlessness, emotional lability, constantly thinking about drugs, and other symptoms which had also turned up on the wives' list. When this list was done, the therapist concluded: "Even the withdrawal symptoms are the same. The only difference is that the addicts were withdrawing from substances and the wives were withdrawing from people. Otherwise, it's the same."

The therapist added one more important similarity: "Now, you've all seen—in fact, *you've* told *me*—how similar the family version of this disease is to the chemical version of it. There's one more way the family disease is the same: You can *die* of it. In fact, it's not at all unusual for family members of chemically dependent people to die of this disease, even if they've never taken a drink or used a drug. There are a number of ways. For example, you can die in an alcohol- or drug-related traffic accident. Or a fire caused by a drunk who passed out while smoking. Or be beaten to death by somebody too high to realize the damage he's doing. Or be shot by a crazed, jealous lover who imagines you're cheating on him. Or die young of an ulcer or stroke brought on by the stress of living with chemical dependency. Or be driven by hopelessness and despair to committing suicide."

The process was nearly complete. The therapist concluded: "Now, can you see now how sick you can get from chemical dependency, even die, just by being married or related to a chemically dependent person?" Heads nodded vigorously in agreement. "Do you see how dangerous and desperate your situation is?" Again heads nodded. "Do you see how badly you need to *do something* about it?" Heads nodded yet again. "Then, what are you going to do about it?"

The rest of the session was devoted to discussing measures the spouses and other family members could take to recover from their disease. Someone mentioned Al-Anon, and the therapist strongly supported that idea. If someone hadn't mentioned it, he would have brought it up anyway. Before the session closed, the therapist requested and got commitments from all family members to attend at least one Al-Anon meeting during the week and to return to the next family session and report on their experiences there. Those without transportation found others willing to give them a ride. Several participants exchanged telephone numbers so that they could share information about meetings, give directions to them, or just call to give or receive support. At last, the meeting ended.

VARIATIONS ON THE THEME

Most family meetings followed the same general outline: an introductory phase, consisting of an attention-getting component and a lecture with a request for a commitment, followed by a group interaction phase in which the therapist called on the participants to exercise the commitments they made in the previous phase. When therapists made variations, they usually changed the method used to get attention, the content of the lecture, or the topic or issue that was discussed in the interaction phase. Sometimes, they shortened or eliminated the introductory phase, which was unnecessary if all or most participants had already attended one session or more; in that case, the therapist needed only to remind the group of its previous commitments, or, better yet, ask participants to state them. Often, they combined the attention-getting and lecture components, which worked well if the lecture began with a "bang."

The rest of this chapter consists of examples of topics that therapists found useful in family sessions, and how they presented the topics. Two of them were designed to reduce or counteract enabling by family members and lovers, one was designed to help participants get out of their denial and face reality honestly, and one illustrates how one participant's tragedy was utilized to help others recover.

How Do You Kill a Drunk?

As one of the primary symptoms of codependency, enabling often proves to be as lethal as drinking and drug use are. To help family members see how lethal it is, the therapist presented the following lecture:

> After seating himself and waiting for silence, the therapist asked the group: "How do you kill a drunk?" He was greeted with silence. He repeated the question: "You heard me. How do you *kill* a drunk?" Again, the group was silent. He continued, "Well, maybe the group needs some help with this one. I don't mean, how do you kill a drunk the way you'd kill someone else, like shooting or stabbing or strangling. I mean something more sneaky. A way of killing where you don't get any blood on your hands. A way of killing where you don't break any laws. A way of killing where you can even tell yourself that you didn't do it, that he did it to himself. Can anyone think of a way to kill a drunk that way?"
>
> Frank, one of the inpatients, raised his hand, and the therapist called on him. "Maybe you could pour him a drink," Frank guessed.
>
> "That's very good, Frank," the therapist observed. "Pouring him a drink *could* kill a drunk. It certainly could. But pouring one drink probably wouldn't be enough to make

sure he dies. To do that, you'd have to pour him a lot of drinks a lot of times. Maybe it would do the trick if you poured him a drink every time he wants one. Is there anybody here who's tried to kill a drunk that way, by pouring him a drink whenever he asks for one?"

The group was silent once again.

The therapist tried again: "O.K., maybe nobody here wants to think of themselves as a cold-blooded killer. So let me ask this: Is there anybody here who poured a drink for her alcoholic whenever he asked, or most of the times he asked? And not to kill him, but just to be nice to him?"

Mrs. Smith raised her hand and admitted that she had poured drinks for her husband. "But I did it just to keep peace in the family. If I hadn't, he would have made life hell for all of us."

The therapist replied: "Well, here's one brave, honest soul. Are there any others who will admit to pouring drinks for their alcoholics?"

Finally, Mrs. Jones raised her hand, and then a handful of others raised theirs.

"Good," the therapist enthused. "There are lots of honest people here tonight. Now let me ask you some more questions. Those of you who raised your hands, were you aware that your alcoholic's drinking was killing him?"

Heads nodded. Mrs. Smith tried to comment: "Yes, but . . ."

The therapist interrupted. "Please hold your explanations and just follow along for a little while. We can deal with reasons why later. So you were aware that his drinking was killing him, but you were giving him drinks anyway. How can you say that you weren't trying to kill him?"

Mrs. Jones had an answer: "If I didn't give it to him, he'd have gotten it somewhere else."

"And why didn't you *let* him get it somewhere else, Mrs. Smith?" the therapist asked.

"I was trying to help him," she answered. "If he went out and got it somewhere else, he might've gotten hurt or hurt someone else. Even though he was drinking, I felt better knowing where he was."

"In other words, you felt better killing him safely at home," the therapist remarked, "than letting him commit suicide somewhere else. Somehow, that doesn't make a lot of sense to me. As I see it, dead is dead, and you were pouring him the stuff that was going to make him that way. But let me ask the group another question. Is pouring a drink the only way to make alcohol available to an alcoholic?"

"No," said Mrs. Brown, who had attended several family meetings before. "You could keep it around the house or go shopping for it."

"That's right, Mrs. Brown," the therapist agreed. "That way, you could make sure he winds up dead, but you could feel more innocent, because he poured his own. All you did was keep his supply up. That's good. Simple but deadly. Is there anyone here who bought alcohol for an alcoholic?"

Hands raised again, more this time than last time. Mrs. Smith interrupted again: "But I wasn't trying to kill him. I was just doing what was expected of me as a wife."

"O.K., Mrs. Smith, I'm willing to believe that you didn't think you were killing him," the therapist conceded. "But his drinking *was* killing him, and *you* were providing the alcohol. And I don't know where it's written that a wife is expected to supply her husband with stuff that's going to kill him. That just doesn't make sense. Can you see that? Can you see how crazy it is?"

Mrs. Smith began to cry as she nodded in reluctant agreement. While other participants comforted her, the therapist continued.

"We've only scratched the surface here," he said. "There are lots more devious ways to kill a drunk than just pouring him a drink or making alcohol available."

The therapist continued with the process of backward communication, leading the group to "discover" the myriad ways a codependent spouse, lover, or relative can enable an alcoholic. Some of these included knowing the alcoholic's drinking is killing him but saying or doing nothing about it; cleaning up the alcoholic's messes, thereby delaying him from facing the consequences of his drinking; bailing him out of jail when he is arrested for a drinking-related offense; criticizing, nagging, "guilt-tripping," commenting on the drinking, or starting arguments; rescuing, fixing, and controlling; and many others. The therapist made sure that each general type of enabling discussed by the group was represented by one or more concrete, specific examples from the participants' lives, and that the group never lost sight of the inevitable "bottom line" of enabling: death. At this point, the therapist might also add stories of past examples of "killing" alcoholics or addicts; this technique is described in greater detail later.

TRAPPING THE SABOTAGING GIRLFRIEND

This example is yet another application of backward communication. In this instance, the behavior of Lisa, the seductive girlfriend of one of the young male patients, lay at the center of the bullseye at which the process aimed. She had met our patient a week prior to his admission and was clinging to him tightly, apparently unaware that falling in love with a freshly diagnosed addicted patient was a risky proposition. The two of them sat in the back of the room, out of the therapist's direct line of sight, but he was aware that they were touching and cuddling and making eyes at each other, and that the patient's ability to concentrate on his treatment was becoming severely impaired.

The therapist considered ignoring the two lovebirds, but decided against that, since his silence could be interpreted as approval of their antics. He considered commenting to or about them directly and immediately, but discarded that option also, as soon as he realized that he could make them and their behavior the main topic of the session in a way that would provide good therapy for the entire group and give them a message they would not soon forget.

The therapist began with an abbreviated version of the example just described, having the group focus on how to kill an addict or alcoholic. He made sure that one of the ways the group came up with to kill an alcoholic or addict was to distract him from his treatment. Once that point was established, he repeated it ominously several times and then shifted to a new topic.

Next, the therapist ran through an abbreviated version of the first example presented: what it is like to be married to an addict or alcoholic. He got wives to tell extremely painful and horrible stories. Meanwhile, he noticed that the two lovebirds were still busy exciting each other, lost in a private world of hand holding, leg rubbing, and perfume smelling, only dimly aware of the topic of discussion.

Finally, the groundwork was laid, and the therapist moved swiftly to close in on the unwitting target of the process. First, he asked each of the wives what advice they would give to any young woman who might be thinking about getting romantically involved with an alcoholic or addict. One after the other, showing considerable emotion as they spoke, they said that their advice to such a young woman would be: "*Don't do it.*"

Then, he slowly and calmly asked: "What do *you* think about that," then loudly and impressively, "Lisa?"

Lisa was shocked. It dawned on her that an entire hour of the therapy session had been spent leading up to this moment, that she had been the target all along. She also realized that every base had been covered and she had nothing to say in her defense. She had been caught "redhanded." She sputtered out an answer, but it was ineffective.

The therapist asked her if she was interested in becoming

romantically involved with an alcoholic or addict. She glanced at her boyfriend, then back at the therapist and nervously said "Yes."

Then, the therapist turned to the wives, who had just described their pain and stated the advice they would give to some abstract young woman headed toward the same kind of peril, and he pointed out that they now had an opportunity to talk to an actual young woman in that situation. "Go ahead," he urged. "Tell Lisa what you think about the path she's about to embark on. Maybe you can put your years of painful experience to some good use."

The remainder of the meeting was consumed by an emotional interchange between Lisa and the wives, with the wives trying every way they could think of to show her the danger of her actions both to herself and to the addicted patient. It soon became obvious that Lisa was in deep denial and was either unwilling or unable to perceive the danger she was in.

The wives learned from this experience a great deal about the strength of denial in their disease of codependency and the inpatient group learned about a major threat to the recovery of their peer, Lisa's boyfriend. Lisa may have learned something too, but she did not admit so during the meeting. Nevertheless, she did not return, either to the family meeting or to become further involved with the patient.

How many kinds of lies are there? Honesty is a very important element in recovery from both chemical dependency and codependency. The Twelve Step programs, including Alcoholics Anonymous and Al-Anon, say that honesty is essential. An illustration of the importance of honesty in A.A. is the fact that the first paragraph of the chapter "How It Works," which introduces the Twelve Steps in the book *Alcoholics Anonymous* (1976), mentions honesty three times and states that the primary stumbling block to recovery is the inability to be honest with oneself.

Keeping this in mind, the therapist began the session with the question:

"How many kinds of lies are there?" He looked around the room, and, seeing no hands raised, addressed one of the participants: "Phil, how about you? I'm sure *you* know something about lies. Tell the group about some of the kinds of lies you've, uh, experienced."

Phil smiled wryly and admitted, "Yeah, I guess I've told my share of lies. O.K., how about *denial*."

The therapist rephrased Phil's example, saying: "You mean, knowing something's true but denying it?" Phil approved that interpretation.

The therapist asked for more kinds of lies from different participants, both inpatients and family members. Gradually, a list of kinds of lies began to emerge, and the therapist asked a volunteer to write them on the board. Participants listed *outright lies* (saying something one knows is not true); *exaggerating* (stretching the truth); *minimizing* (making something bad seem not so bad); and "*little white lies*."

The therapist said, "That's good. Now, how about telling a lie without ever saying anything that isn't true?" The group came up with *lies of omission*. The therapist asked, "You mean, leaving out important little details, like robbing a bank, and then, when someone asks you where you got the money, you just say you got it at the bank?" Then, he continued, asking for other ways someone could lie while telling the truth.

The group came up with telling the truth about someone, but *having a dishonest motive*. The therapist clarified that kind of lie by saying, "Oh. After you've ruined someone's reputation, gotten them fired and divorced and discredited, you excuse it by saying, 'Well, it's true.' Yeah, that's a great lie. Here's another kind: How about *lying on credit*?"

The group had no idea what the therapist was talking about, but finally, with hints, realized that he meant *promises*. "That's right," he said. "You can tell a lie, and it stays true for the longest time, right up to a certain date or time, and then it's just as false as anything. Remember how Wimpy used to promise Popeye that he'd gladly repay him on

Tuesday for a hamburger today? That thing stayed true until midnight Tuesday. Then it turned instantly into a lie, just like Cinderella's coach turned into a pumpkin.

"There's a special kind of lying on credit, a special kind of promise, that lots of you know about. In fact, some of you are probably experts. Can you think of what I mean?" No one answered. Finally, he said: "You'll recognize it just as soon as I say it: *threats*! Remember? 'If you ever drink again, I'll leave you.' He did and you didn't. But it was true right up until you found out that he drank. Sound familiar?" Participants had to admit that it did.

The group continued to generate more types of lies, and all were written on the blackboard. The therapist praised the group for knowing so much about lying and for being willing to share its secrets. Then, he asked, "Has anyone ever noticed that you have to tell two lies to tell one? That's right. You have to tell yourself that it's O.K. to tell the lie you're about to tell, and that's a lie too. So you can't just tell one lie." The group agreed.

Then the therapist pointed out that "Once you've told somebody a lie, you're going to have to tell another one pretty soon to cover up that one. So, you see, that's four lies already—the one you tell yourself, the one you tell, and the two you have to tell to cover up the first two. Do you see how fast the lies add up?" The group agreed with that point also, so the therapist went on to the next point.

He asked: "Have any of you ever told so many lies that you couldn't tell for sure which things you told were true and which things you made up?" Many participants, who had been becoming more spirited during the discussion and were laughing about the different types of lies and the examples, nodded vigorously in agreement. The therapist asked: "And do you know what that's called?" No one knew, so the therapist answered his own question. "Insanity. That's called insanity. When you don't know the difference between reality and fantasy, you're insane. And how do you get insane? You lie your way there. It doesn't take much, either. You just start with one little lie and, before you know it, they've multiplied, and multiplied some more, and soon you're insane."

As that conclusion sank in, the therapist moved on to another startling fact. First, he asked: "Do you think you've come up with just about every kind of lie there is? Are you pretty much satisfied with the list?" The group indicated that it was satisfied. Then, he announced, "That's too bad, because you've left out an entire category of lie. I'm surprised. All you've talked about so far is *telling lies.* You've left out one of the most important kinds of lies there is: *living lies.* Do you realize that it's technically possible for someone to live his whole life without ever telling a single lie, but still have his whole life based on a lie?"

The session continued with members coming up with more kinds of lies of both the telling and the living varieties; describing their own personal experiences of lying and being lied to; and discovering and coming to fuller understandings of both the destructive nature of lying and the importance of honesty for recovery.

Utilizing a suicide and group indecision. The last example portrays a therapist's utilization of a tragic event in the life of one of the participants to enhance the therapeutic process in a family group and also to help the participant cope with the tragedy.

Gilda was the wife of a former inpatient. She had attended the family session religiously while her husband was in the program and had subsequently become quite active in Al-Anon. Things had not gone so well for her husband. Not long after he graduated from the program, he relapsed into heavy drinking. Gilda decided that she had had enough of his drinking and divorced him. Unfortunately, he refused to accept losing her and spent a good deal of his time, drunk or sober—but mostly drunk, calling her on the telephone, visiting her at work, and driving by her home at night.

Gilda could not dismiss her ex-husband's calls and visits as mere irritations, because he frequently threatened her. He told her, in effect, that, if he could not have her, no one would; that he would rather see her dead than divorced from him. She knew that he had the means to kill her, because he owned guns and knew how to use them. When threatening her, he made frequent reference to the guns.

Gilda spent several years living in fear. She lay awake at night thinking that every pair of headlights of cars driving by might be her ex-husband come to shoot her. She made escape plans and established a network of friends and relatives to warn her in case he actually came to carry out his threat.

One night, Gilda's telephone rang, and she received a warning that her ex-husband was on his way over with his gun. He had just gotten out of jail for a drunk driving arrest and was enraged that she had not come to bail him out. She dressed hastily and rushed out the back door. Within a few minutes, he arrived and broke in the front door. He was carrying his gun and had come to shoot her and then kill himself. Discouraged that he did not find her, and crazed from despair, jealousy, and alcohol, he shot himself anyway.

Gilda came to the hospital on a Tuesday evening not long after her ex-husband's suicide seeking support and relief. She asked if she could attend the session, even though she was not related to any of the inpatients. The therapist said it would probably be O.K. and that she should attend, but he would have to ask the group for final approval.

The session began in the usual way and it became apparent quite early that several new family members were full of denial about the seriousness of their problems. The therapist raised the subject of how seriously chemical dependency affects the nonaddicted spouse and other family members, and asked several participants how they had been affected.

The new family members looked on smugly as other participants spoke. Then the therapist asked Gilda the same
question.

Gilda told her entire story, leaving out few details. For
example, she pointed out that, after the police and coroner
had left, she had to clean up her living room all alone. No
one was there to help her wash her ex-husband's brains off
the wall. No one was there to support her as she picked his
teeth out of the carpet. She told of her granddaughter's
pathetic comment: "Now grandpa won't fall down over my
doll house any more." She interrupted her story several times
to sob. The emotions were contagious. Soon, everyone in the
room was crying.

The new family members who had been full of denial
could no longer shut out the reality of their situation. Gilda's
story brought the horror of chemical dependency too close
to home. While crying right along with everyone else, they
told their stories of suffering and degradation. A feeling of
unity in suffering filled the room. Denial and resistance evap-
orated. When the session ended, everyone who had partic-
ipated in it was exhausted and yet exhilarated. Just before
the group ended, the therapist mentioned that the group
would have to make a decision about whether Gilda could be
allowed to continue to attend. The group hastily approved
her return the following week.

The next week, Gilda appeared as expected. The group
was still affected by her story, but not quite as strongly.
Nevertheless, talking about her tragedy seemed to be helping
Gilda and her presence in the group kept the focus on feelings and the reality of the disease. Again, the therapist mentioned the need for the group to decide about whether Gilda
should attend, only he brought up the subject earlier this
time than he had the previous week. Again the group
approved her return with no reservations.

This pattern continued for several more weeks, but some
changes occurred. Gilda no longer seemed to be getting the

kind or quality of support she needed and the group seemed to be making her into a mascot instead of using her presence to remain open to feelings and the reality of chemical dependency. The therapist felt that it was time for a change.

He once again raised the issue of whether the group should let Gilda stay or leave, but this time he brought up reasons for not letting her stay that the group could not ignore. Was the group enabling her? Was the group establishing an unhealthy precedent by allowing someone to attend the group who was not related to inpatients, thereby taking up therapy that inpatients and their families should be receiving? Was the group avoiding its own issues by focusing on hers?

The group was in a quandary. All participants were fond of Gilda and felt quite sorry for her. They did not want to lose her and they did not want to hurt her by rejecting her. But they also saw that by allowing her to stay they might be violating important principles that could reduce the effectiveness of both their therapy and hers.

This new question raised anxieties considerably. No one wanted to make the decision in either direction. As the group struggled, the therapist let the tide of opinion sweep one way and then the other. If the group seemed to be near a decision, the therapist argued for the other side. The level of emotion reached a fever pitch and remained there.

Just as was often the case with chemical dependency group meetings, the group become focused on which decision it would make, forgetting the overall experience of therapy. The therapist was content to keep the group undecided, because it was now back in touch with feelings and with the reality of the disease. As the group careened wildly back and forth between deciding to keep Gilda and thrusting her out, the therapist identified for the group many of the dynamics of chemical dependency and codependency as they appeared in the group's behavior: the tendency to enable; the difficulty assuming responsibility; the difficulty facing and dealing with emotion; the life-or-death nature of the disease. In addition, he saw to it that the group experienced as much emotion as possible instead of denying or suppressing it, so that all participants could learn how to tolerate their feelings.

The session ended without a decision. The following week, the group tried to ignore the fact that it had failed to decide and attempted to act as if it had decided. The therapist would not let this pass without comment and soon the process of the preceding week was in full swing. The group was still in a quandary, emotions continued to run high, and excellent therapy was had by all. Still, the group ended without a decision.

This process continued for one or two more sessions, then was resolved by the fact that Gilda simply stopped showing up. The group moved on to other topics.

This example demonstrates how therapists can utilize events and conditions to increase the value of therapy. The event of Gilda's ex-husband's suicide helped the group immeasurably. It was easy for the therapist to use that event. When that event ceased to be effective, and a new condition emerged, the therapist found a way to utilize the new condition to keep the therapeutic effectiveness going for several more weeks.

STORYTELLING

One of Erickson's favorite therapy and teaching methods was to tell stories that both served as illustrations of points he wanted to get across and contained implied suggestions that listeners could easily accept because of the nonthreatening nature of the interaction, i.e., just listening to stories.

Two stories that proved to be very useful in dealing with family issues were the stories of Jim and Mary, and of Dan and Alice. Both concerned women who sabotaged their chemically dependent husbands' treatment, and they were useful as illustrations when teaching family members about enabling. They also were useful in helping chemically dependent patients understand the family issues they were likely to face upon discharge from treatment. Finally, they helped prevent family members from enabling, because they "took away" certain behaviors as options, much as predicting or prescribing symptoms might do, and they contained a great deal of emotional impact, which was intensified by their being told dramatically. Another way to use these stories might be to tie them in to other techniques or themes, such as the "How do you kill a drunk?" script given earlier in this chapter.

Following one of Jim,'s worst drinking sprees, which left him very ill and nearly broke, his wife Mary took him to the hospital for alcoholism treatment. He began to take part in the program reluctantly at first, but his commitment to recovery became stronger as he realized the extent of his addiction, the life-or-death nature of his situation, and his level of alcohol-related pain. Mary visited Jim often, talked to him on the telephone daily to give him support and encouragement, and expected him to call her daily with reports of his progress.

At first, the telephone calls and visits were routine. However, as the days passed, Mary called more often and kept Jim on the phone for longer periods. Her emotional tone changed too, from gently supportive to distraught and panicky. Jim talked about Mary's calls in group therapy sessions and it was obvious that the calls disturbed him a great deal. His tension increased daily as the intensity of Mary's calls escalated.

Mary began by telling Jim—in her sexiest, most seductive voice—how much she missed him and wished he were home. Wasn't he well enough yet to come home? Didn't he miss her, too? In spite of his temptation to come home, he told her that the program staff had explained to him that he was just beginning to recover and would need to stay a lot longer than one week. Besides, he added, he was sick and tired of drinking and all the associated problems, and he really wanted to get well this time.

Mary's second call was not pleading and tempting like the first. This time, she sounded helpless, troubled, and in need of rescue. The lawn hadn't been mowed, the faucets were leaking, the bills were piling up, and the children were misbehaving. She just couldn't handle all these problems alone. Wouldn't he please come home and help her? Once again he apologized and reaffirmed his commitment to stay in the program and get well. He found it difficult to tell her this, because he felt extremely guilty about having neglected his responsibilities while drinking. He felt a strong urge to make the guilt go away by rushing home and making it all up to her. He discussed these feelings in group and was able to strengthen his resolve to complete treatment.

Mary's complaints next shifted from worries about minor inconveniences to concern about ominous-sounding emergencies. Now she was worried about Jimmy Junior's nosebleed that wouldn't stop and little Sally's turned ankle, maybe it was broken! She was so beside herself, she told him, that she had begun having accidents. While driving home from her job. she had a frighteningly close call with one car and actually hit another car a few minutes later; fortunately, the damages were minor—this time. She was worried that "something awful" might happen while Jim was in the hospital and she would feel so much safer if he were home. Again, Jim overcame his temptation to rush to the rescue, but his resolve was beginning to weaken.

Then, Mary's tone changed again. Sounding unexpectedly calm and secure, even a bit bubbly, she told Jim that she knew she was going to be fine now. She had had a long talk with a recently divorced man at work. He seemed so understanding and thoughtful, and he offered to help her around the house while Jim was away. In fact, she was going over to his place that evening for dinner and drinks.

No sooner had Jim hung up the telephone than he was

packing his suitcase and heading out the door. He was overcome by jealousy and felt compelled to keep his wife away
from the "other man." Although members of his group gathered around him and used every argument they could think
of to dissuade him from leaving, Jim refused to listen. He
broke through their ranks and disappeared.

A few days later, we received a call from Mary, who complained that Jim had been drinking again. When we suggested that she bring him to the hospital so that he could
complete treatment, she responded that she would be able to
help him by herself and all she needed was a few helpful
hints. We never saw either of them again, but a few weeks
later she contacted the medical records department and
demanded his admission and discharge notes and then complained about something one of the notes said about her.
Later, there were a few rumors about his drinking getting
much worse and her walking out on the marriage as he lay
passed out on their living room floor.

Another patient's spouse had a similar reaction, but she was
much less subtle about it than Mary had been:

Within three or four days after dropping off her husband,
Dan, for alcoholism treatment, Alice made a series of telephone calls to the program director and medical director. She
wanted to have special arrangements made for visiting,
which, if they had been granted, would have completely dis-
rupted the program schedule. She also demanded detailed
reports from the staff about Dan's progress in the program.
When it was made clear to her that we could not accommodate her requests in order not to endanger the integrity of
the program, she abruptly terminated the telephone conversation and appeared a short time later at the hospital. There,
she repeated her demands in a loud and insistent manner.
When again she failed to get her way, she announced that she
was taking Dan with her, ostensibly to enroll him in another

program she said she had picked out. We told her that it was our understanding that Dan wanted to stay in the program he was in and it could be harmful to his recovery to move him at that time. Still she insisted and became more and more extreme and irrational in her demands. Finally, we agreed to have a special meeting with her and Dan and the entire patient group early the next morning.

Alice entered the group therapy room in a hostile, defiant manner and waited impatiently for everyone to be seated. When the meeting was called to order, she restated her demand that Dan leave treatment and go with her. When asked how he felt about leaving the program, Dan stated that he wanted to stay, even if Alice didn't like it. Suddenly she pulled a packet of papers from her large purse, stomped dramatically across the room, and threw the papers in Dan's lap. "These are divorce papers. I'm serving you. But I'll drop the whole thing if you come with me now." Dan went with her.

6

Some Final Reflections

The first five chapters convey the bulk of the "message" this book was designed to communicate. This chapter contains an assortment of reflections and afterthoughts. Most of these ideas are comments on, extensions of, or caveats about the clinical methods presented and their implications.

THE VALUE OF THE TWELVE STEPS

I cannot emphasize strongly enough how valuable the Twelve Steps and Twelve Step programs are in recovery from addictions.

The Steps themselves offer what amounts to a practical theoretical system that is comprehensible to both therapist and patient, thus providing an excellent language for communicating about the processes of therapy and recovery. When both patient and therapist are well versed in Twelve Step "lingo," they can forego the time-consuming process of teaching and learning psychological concepts and establish communication as quickly and easily as two members of a culture meeting in a foreign land.

The theory underlying the Twelve Steps is remarkably sophisticated from a psychological point of view. I remember being quite surprised to learn of the important roles played in the formation of Alcoholics Anonymous by such figures as Carl Jung and William James, as well as subsequent contributions by the psychoanalytically oriented psychiatrist Harry Tiebout and anthropologist Gregory Bateson, among others. There is an implicit notion of unconscious processes in the Twelve Steps, but it little resembles Freud's vision of the unconscious. Instead, it seems to fit remarkably well with Erickson's understanding of unconscious change. That opens up Erickson's entire "kit" of therapy techniques for the field of addiction.

Many therapists view the Twelve Step programs as an excellent source of support for their patients and a valuable adjunct to therapy. I go a step further and view the Twelve Step programs as the *primary* therapy for addictions, with my services and the services provided by addiction treatment programs being adjunctive to them. In other words, our job is to do all we can to ensure that our patients make maximum use of and derive maximum benefit from the Twelve Step programs.

Some therapists seem to view Twelve Step programs as if they were competitors, and unfair competitors at that, because they are nonprofessional (and therefore inferior) and charge nothing for their services. Let me assure anyone who may agree with this view that it is completely inaccurate. There are plenty of addicted people to go around and there would be more than enough for every therapist in the world even if Twelve Step programs really did steal or keep their members away from therapists. However, my experience has been that Twelve Step programs actually create more patients for therapists. After working on their various issues for a time in Twelve Step programs, many members discover a need for therapy that they would otherwise have overlooked, since they would have been too immersed in active addiction to even notice their problems if they had never gone to Twelve Step recovery programs. It is clear that many addicted people have problems other than addiction for which therapy can be beneficial. They, therefore, need to find therapists who can understand and appreciate Twelve Step programs. In addition, patients very rarely feel compelled to choose between therapy and Twelve Step programs. They much more commonly do both concurrently. I have found that psychotherapy with patients who are also involved in a Twelve Step program tends to be much more rewarding than it is with patients who are not involved in one.

I have one final thought on Twelve Step programs. If you are working in the addiction field or if you are working with a lot of addicted people, regardless of the field you identify with, you should give serious consideration to becoming a member of a Twelve Step program yourself. If you don't qualify for one of the programs because of not being addicted to alcohol or drugs or cigarettes or overeating, then you might qualify because of being related to someone who is. Failing that, you are certainly "related" to your patients who are addicted; on that basis alone, you qualify for Al-Anon. Then, there are Neurotics Anonymous, Emotions Anonymous, and Emotional Health Anonymous, where participants admit to being powerless over their emotions.

I am not taking the "hard-line" position that you can't help an addicted person if you aren't one. I'm not even taking the position that you can't help someone in a Twelve Step program if you aren't in one. Joining a Twelve Step program probably will help you to understand and help your addicted patients at least a little better. Above all, joining a Twelve Step program will probably help you to understand and help *yourself* a little better.

OTHER ADDICTIONS AND TREATMENT MODALITIES

I am so enthused by the application of Erickson-inspired techniques to chemical dependency that I want to point out other, related problems that can be treated with these methods, as well as other settings and modalities where they can be employed.

A number of addictions and compulsive behavior problems have been or can be successfully addressed with Twelve Step programs and addiction treatment methods, so they are also quite likely to benefit from the Erickson-inspired techniques described in this book and from similar methods that may arise from the creative minds of other Erickson-inspired addictions therapists. These problems are cigarette smoking or nicotine addiction; compulsive overeating and eating disorders; codependency, adult children of alcoholics issues, or relationship or love addiction; compulsive sexual behaviors or sexual addiction; and compulsive or pathological gambling.

Treatment techniques or settings that can incorporate or benefit from Erickson-inspired methods include interventions; lectures or patient education; activities therapy; art therapy; occupational therapy; music, dance, or movement therapy; milieu therapy; therapeutic communities; prisons; and halfway or recovery homes. I'm sure that there are others I have neglected to mention.

ETHICAL CONSIDERATIONS

The techniques I have described in this volume are powerful. Whenever there are powerful techniques, there is heightened risk; therefore, important ethical considerations arise. The questions I want to bring up concern the use and abuse of power and the issue of manipulation versus free will.

Use and Abuse of Power

Extraordinary problems require extraordinary solutions. Addiction is an extremely powerful disease. Accepting this fact, I have worked hard to find and develop the most powerful possible treatment techniques. I offer them with some hesitancy, since these and similar techniques could be abused. The more powerful they are, the more devastating the results of their abuse could be. I think that the risk is acceptable because of the greater good that can come from treating addictions effectively. I also think that not offering powerful techniques because of their potential for abuse might be more unethical than offering them and taking the risk.

In any case, I want to list the kinds of risks that I regard as most dangerous and to suggest how to avoid them.

Potential risks from use of these techniques could affect both recipients of services (patients or clients) and providers (therapists or counselors). The biggest risks to recipients would come as the result of providers' using the techniques to gain power for themselves, in essence by forming personality cults. Another risk can arise from verbal abuse or other callous disregard of recipients' feelings. The greatest risks to providers would arise from their coming to see themselves as infallible and/or as personality cult leaders themselves.

The primary purposes these techniques were designed to accomplish are to open recipients up to the potential for change that resides within themselves and to acquaint them with sound principles that, if followed, will lead them to recovery from their devastating illnesses.

Unethical providers or leaders could ignore these goals and use the same techniques to draw and bind recipients or followers to them to increase their own power and influence. We would prefer to think that this kind of cult leadership occurs only outside the therapy and treatment community. Doubtless, there are plenty of such people out in the world and some of them probably study therapy methods, hoping to sharpen their manipulation skills. There are also people with similar leanings inside the therapy and treatment community, as evidenced by the frequency with which therapists seduce their patients or otherwise take advantage of patients' dependence and vulnerability.

Another source of risk to recipients is the possibility of verbal abuse or degradation. The methods described here often employ confrontation, pressure, sarcasm, discussion of sensitive issues, humor, parody, and "telling it like it is." Any of these forms of communication could be extremely hurtful to the fragile ego of a suffering chemically dependent person if delivered in just slightly the wrong way. For the large subgroup of these patients who suffered from severe child abuse, verbal abuse by a therapist or counselor would constitute not only present abuse but also re-abuse, because it could unexpectedly trigger revivification of old abuse experiences and cause patients to run away from treatment and refuse to seek needed help ever again.

The danger to providers of services is somewhat more subtle. Therapists or counselors who become adept at influencing individuals or groups could begin to believe themselves infallible. Power and influence can be very seductively rewarding, particularly so for a therapist or counselor who has an outsized craving to be loved, admired, and respected. The situation is similar to that of a bank employee desperately in need of money who sees thousands of dollars in cash pass before him or her daily. At times, the temptation may be overwhelming to reach for a little bit of it. By doing so, a bank employee would be embarking on a life of crime. Similarly, therapists or counselors who go for the power and start their own cults would be plunging themselves into the contradictory, dishonest, and eventually untenable position of pretending to serve others while actually becoming more and more self-serving. And they could easily rationalize their behavior as it progresses in this direction until the process becomes irreversible.

What can be done to prevent these dangers? First of all, nothing can be done to prevent persons outside the therapeutic community from reading psychotherapy books and becoming proficient manipulators, unless they break laws. Persons inside the treatment community who might be tempted to recruit cult followers are subject to codes of ethics and fears of losing jobs, licenses, and careers. But fears of negative sanctions are not enough, especially when one considers the seductive power of the reinforcements available to professionals who master these techniques. The best preventive measures are consistent supervision, psychotherapy and/or Twelve Step program membership for therapists, and commitment on the part of therapists to promoting conformance by patients to principles rather than to personalities.

To prevent verbal abuse of patients, therapists and counselors can follow some simple guidelines. First, never insult patients directly or make them butts of jokes; only insult "a person like . . . ," "somebody who . . . ," or an entire group. Second, only insult for therapeutic reasons, not just because it feels good, and make sure that the therapeutic reason you tell yourself is not just a rationalization. Third, only insult if you are certain that there is loving support in the peer group for the implied recipient or recipients of the insult. Finally, do not even use techniques involving possible verbal abuse—or the possibility that any patient will take what you are saying as abuse, whether intended as such or not—unless you are prepared to deal clinically with the revivifications of childhood abuse that might be evoked.

MANIPULATION VS. FREE WILL

Should a therapist be a manipulator? This question is complicated by the negative value tone often associated with the term "manipulator." In an effort to neutralize this effect, let me rephrase the question as follows: Should a therapist actively attempt to change a patient's or group's behavior in a direction chosen by the therapist, or should the therapist act only as a facilitator or midwife to whatever emerges from the patient or group and leave the course of change up to the patient or group to decide? Or, to use a botanical metaphor, with a patient's growth or change being represented by a plant: Should a therapist prune or stake or direct the growth of the plant in a deliberate manner or simply supply sunshine and water so that the potential inner essence of the plant will emerge as it will?

My position on this question may seem paradoxical: I am strongly in favor of both free will *and* manipulation. However, the paradox is only a seeming one, as I hope my explanation makes clear. It is my ultimate goal for chemically dependent patients that they eventually become completely free. Yet, I believe that it is often necessary to be directive and manipulative to help them achieve this freedom.

The sunshine and water metaphor is deceptively nice and comfortable and leaves out an important element: the fact that the plant (that is, the patient) has a bigger problem than simply a lack

of sunshine and water. It (he or she) is actively under attack by a
pathological process, addiction, that is already busily at work
pruning and staking and directing the plant (patient) in a destructive and eventually fatal manner. If someone doesn't actively intervene in this situation, by stopping and redirecting the pathological
process, the plant (patient) is a goner.

The laissez-faire attitude of traditional psychotherapists makes
them ineffective when they are faced with addicted patients.
Addiction thrives on being allowed to do whatever it wants. It finds
ways of making anyone or anything that isn't part of the solution
become part of the problem. That is why traditional, insight-
oriented, psychodynamic psychotherapists become enablers of the
worst sort. Addicts can go to them for years, keep drinking and
using the whole time, and proudly proclaim to anyone who objects
to their drinking or drug problems that they are "doing something about it."

Many psychotherapists were trained to back off, be reflective,
help patients grow, and keep from imposing their own values on
them. No wonder we find it hard to think of ourselves as manipulators. We need to change this almost reflexive stance if we are
going to help addicted patients. We need to feel secure and
unapologetic about being manipulators. Other health professionals manipulate with no difficulty whatsoever. For example, surgeons perform extremely manipulative and directive procedures
on their patients. If they don't feel guilty about wielding scalpels,
we shouldn't feel guilty about using directive, strategic therapy
techniques.

ADDICTION AND DISSOCIATION

Dissociative phenomena are common occurrences in connection
with chemical use and chemical dependency; some of them are
very important to an understanding of the disease and the process
of recovery. The subject of dissociation takes on added importance
in connection with a discussion of Erickson-inspired techniques

because of Erickson's emphasis on unconscious processes and hypnosis in psychotherapy. This section contains some observations and hypotheses about connections between addiction and dissociation.

I originally noticed three types of dissociative experiences in chemical dependency settings. One is the transformation that occurs in chemically dependent people during the first few doses of a chemical. Another is the appearance of ego-states in chronic chemically dependent people. Finally, there is the phenomenon I call the "dry drunk."

THE TRANSFORMATION

A woman told me that her drinking pattern was to go to a bar that had a mirror so that she could watch the change take place as she "drank herself beautiful." Such Walter Mitty-like transformations are very common among chemically dependent people. Those who are shy and fearful transform themselves into confident and brave. Those who are dull and drab transform themselves into exciting and colorful. Army privates transform themselves into colonels, automobile mechanics transform themselves into singing stars, waitresses become movie queens, and salesmen become major corporate executives, brain surgeons, or nuclear physicists.

Chronic high levels of emotional pain and low self-worth cause chemically dependent people to want to escape from themselves and become someone or something good, important, and valuable. Simply *feeling* different is not enough after awhile; they seem to need to take on a different identity. Alcohol and drugs allow them to suspend their critical faculties so that they can *live* their fantasies for awhile, instead of just fantasizing them. Many chemically dependent people live these fantasy roles so fully that their style of dress changes, their manner of speaking and acting changes, and they assume an alias.

It is interesting to note that these transformations can occur in the absence of chemicals. Compulsive gamblers are one group that achieves a similar transformation through an activity alone. Gamblers usually transform themselves from ordinary, lackluster citizens into "high rollers," masters of the blackjack table, or possessors of the "ultimate" handicapping system. They get high on the "action" in such a way that they seem drugged by it. They are captured by their roles and keep playing them until they find themselves deeply in debt. In fact, the role and the action seem to be the main incentive for continued gambling, much more so than any winnings the gamblers may accumulate, because winnings are not spent or saved—they are used to keep the action going.

EGO-STATES

Chemically dependent people often behave as though they have an ego-state (Watkins, 1984; Watkins & Johnson, 1982) that contains unacceptable emotions and impulses and strives for control of their behavior by getting them drunk or high. This entity, which Horn and I (Horn & Lovern, 1981) originally called *the hated self*, appears to operate from an unconscious hiding place, where it watches and waits for opportunities to accomplish its task by cleverly manipulating the person into drinking and using drugs. We conceived of a number of the therapeutic techniques mentioned earlier—particularly those that aroused strong negative emotions—as methods for activating the hated self so that he or she could receive therapy, instead of limiting it to just the more "nice" and cooperative sides of our patients.

THE DRY DRUNK

One meaning of the popularly used term "dry drunk" refers to a *person* who, although not drinking, still behaves the way he or she did while drinking: "I wasn't recovering; I was just a dry drunk." Another meaning refers to a *state* resembling intoxication that takes over a person's behavior even if he or she has not been drinking: "He went on a really bad dry drunk last night." When I talk about dry drunks, I am referring to the state, not the person.

Dry drunk states occur spontaneously, with no obvious warning and with little or no awareness by the person of the changed state. Usually, the person becomes moody or sullen and seems a bit dreamy and disconnected. As the change progresses, the person begins to be dominated by an emotion. Often, the emotion is anger, but it can be others, such as anxiety, fear, sadness, or silliness. The person begins to behave strangely: He or she seems to have "copped an attitude" and is combative, stubborn, or irritable. The person is also unreachable and will not discuss what is happening within him- or herself.

If the dry drunk continues, the next stage is an eruption of inappropriate or extreme behavior. The person panics, breaks into tears, flies into a rage, becomes verbally or physically abusive, and/or gets drunk or uses drugs, as is most often the case in the absence of a strong recovery-supporting system. Dry drunks usually lead to wet drunks.

After the fact, patients commonly describe the experience as one in which they felt as if there were two of themselves, with one watching the other as it behaved irrationally and feeling that it should do something to stop or change the behavior of the other one, but at the same time feeling strangely unconcerned and lethargic. They also occasionally describe distorted perceptions or hallucinations, with dim recollection of or complete inability to recall events that occurred during the dry drunk episode. Thus, there are "dry hallucinations" and "dry blackouts." After the episode—usually the morning after, but only if they did not drink or use drugs—many people experience a form of "dry hangover": headaches, guilt and self-recrimination, exhaustion, and a dazed, disconnected feeling.

During an inpatient session, the group was struggling and bickering over some small detail of a plan it was working on. Suddenly, John, whose job it was to take minutes of the proceedings, jumped up from his seat, shouted that he had had it and could not "take this bullshit anymore," threw his tablet and pencil on the floor, and stormed out of the room. As soon as he left, the entire group rose to its feet and followed him to his room, where he was found throwing wads of clothing and other personal belongings helter-skelter into a suitcase on his bed. Members of the group gathered around him and gently told him that they wanted him to stay and were afraid that he might go out and get drunk if he left. He shouted at them, made menacing gestures, and insisted that they get back and leave him alone.

Eventually, the group managed to calm John down somewhat and talk him into unpacking and coming back to the meeting room. He continued to be agitated and belligerent, but agreed to stay until morning. The group decided that John needed special help the rest of the day and during the night, so it voted to place him on "dry detox"—that is, he traded his street clothes for pajamas and two fellow patients stayed with him at all times until the crisis passed.

The following morning, John's appearance and demeanor were completely different. He was calm and agreeable, complained of a headache, and wanted to apologize to the group and the staff. He said that he couldn't remember everything he had done the day before, but he knew he had been difficult. He said that the other patients who had gathered around him to try to help, didn't even look like people: "They were little green men, just little green men." He was surprised that he had acted in a manner so uncharacteristic of himself and was appalled that he had been unable to control his behavior. "I just couldn't stop. I wanted to, but I couldn't."

Another dry drunk that occurred in a treatment context provides a dramatic example of a memory blackout:

During an outpatient-couple-therapy group, Al, who had not had a drink for at least a year, suddenly and unexpectedly bolted from the therapy room after taking offense at an innocuous remark by one of the other patients. Not only did he leave the therapy room, but he stormed out of the hospital and walked several blocks before slowing down. The other group members attempted to follow him and found that he was moving so fast that some of them had to drive their cars to keep him in sight. They finally caught up with him on a street corner, where he was pacing back and forth restlessly, with a wild look in his eyes.

The group gathered around Al and tried to find out what was troubling him, why he had left the therapy session, and how they might be able to help. He failed to respond in any way. He simply kept pacing and scanning the street around him, behaving as if he was completely unaware of the presence of the other group members. After a few moments, Al spotted a police patrol car. Something about it jolted him back to his normal consciousness. He became aware of the people around him for the first time and asked, "Where am I? What am I doing here?"

POST-TRAUMATIC STRESS AND MULTIPLE PERSONALITY DISORDER

Since originally observing the phenomena described above, I have learned a great deal about dissociation and dissociative disorders, and as I look back on the original observations, I notice that they seem rather naive. The new information that sheds valuable light on the relationship between addiction and dissociation concerns post-traumatic stress and multiple personality disorder.

First, it is important to point out that dissociative disorders, and multiple personalities, in particular, are not rare. Since learning how to identify patients with multiple personality disorder (MPD), I have found that approximately a third of my patients, most of whom had originally sought help only for chemical dependency and/or eating disorders, clearly qualify for the diagnosis of multiple personality disorder.

The high proportion of patients with MPD in my practice is not the result of patients being referred to me because they have the disorder, since all cases arose from the ranks of patients referred for other problems. Neither is it the result of "multiple personality fever," that is, a tendency on my part to overdiagnose the disorder, since I am intentionally conservative in applying the diagnosis. The high proportion apparently exists simply because many addicted and eating-disordered people also have multiple personality disorder.

Other clinicians who specialize in the treatment of multiple personality disorder have told me anecdotally that a great many of their patients are dependent on alcohol or drugs, or are obese or have eating disorders. In addition, Coons (1984) reported that multiple personality disorder "is strongly associated with alcohol and/or drug abuse," and that "it is not uncommon for patients to have been labeled alcoholic or to have been in an inpatient alcohol program before the diagnosis of multiple personality was made" (page 59). Both Sanders (1986) and Torem (1986, 1987) noted a strong element of dissociation in patients with eating disorders. Torem theorized that the self-starvation of anorexics and the binge eating and purging of bulimics can often be traced back to dissociated "warring and disharmonious ego-states [which are] fighting for executive control" (Torem, 1987). It is fairly clear that a strong connection exists between multiple personality disorder and addictions (and eating disorders). If this connection is true and generalized, why is it so?

The likely connecting link between chemical dependency, eating disorders, and multiple personality disorder is *child abuse*. It is hypothesized that these disorders may represent attempts by victims of child abuse or other early trauma to defend themselves against both the overwhelming stress that occurred at the time of the original trauma and the subsequent stress that occurs when they are troubled by intrusive recollections of the original abuse.

Dissociation, or "out of body experience" (Spiegel, 1984), appears to be the preferred defense employed by intelligent and highly hypnotizable young child victims of severe and repeated abuse or neglect who have no other means of escape (Stern, 1984).

When a child employs dissociation in this way, two major consequences occur: (a) The act of dissociating interrupts the processing of the experience into normal memory, leaving a "chunk" of experience to be lived through as if it were real at some later date when the victim finally finishes processing it. Or else it may be only partially and incompletely processed, leaving the victim with the burden of having to relive "pieces" or aspects of the traumatic event each time he or she encounters stimuli which trigger them. (b) While the child is "away," that is, dissociated or out of body, a separate, split-off part of psychic energy or mental processing remains and may eventually develop an identity of its (or her or his) own.

The processing of events into memory may be seen as occurring in two stages. The first stage is the reception of stimuli; the second stage is the processing or "filing" of these received stimuli into permanent memory storage. Conscious experiencing of an event occurs only during the second, or filing, stage. When people dissociate during traumatic events, they interrupt the mental processing of those events between the first and second stages, leaving the events both incompletely processed and not yet consciously experienced.

When an intrusive recollection of a traumatic event is triggered, a victim may experience it as a complete revivification, as one component, or as a combination of components of the experience. The components are Behavior, Affect, Sensation, and Knowledge (Braun's BASK model: Braun, 1986). Thus, a person may act out the original event; feel the emotions that he or she felt at the time; experience a pain, pressure, or other physical sensation; or have knowledge of what occurred. The person may have all of these components together or just one or a few of them without the others. For example, the person might feel strong emotion only (such as terror) or a mysterious head- or abdominal ache, or both together. The "chunks" of experience, their intrusive recollection, and myriad problems arising from the intrusions and attempts to ward them off constitute the syndrome of post-traumatic stress disorder (PTSD).

The split-off part of the child's psychic energy, which is left in the body with the trauma when the child dissociates, develops its own sense of identity if it is employed often enough to have a personal history. It then becomes the first of what are likely to be a number of alternate personalities. From this beginning, the syndrome of multiple personality disorder evolves.

As children grow up subjected to continuing abuse while retaining dissociation as a primary defense, they weave very complex and creative schemes of self-protection. However, no matter how many diverse or specialized personalities they create, they continue to be haunted by the "memories" long after the abuse has stopped. Some alternate personalities are particularly terrified by the memories because they are unable to tell the difference between them and present reality, mistakenly assuming that they are actually being traumatized each time certain memories begin to "play." Many also feel duty bound to protect one or more other personalities from the pain and terror, adding to the pressure to escape or "turn off" the memories. Victims consequently feel a strong need for methods they might employ to supplement and/or strengthen their defenses.

Strategies for warding off the memories. In their efforts to ward off terrifying replays of traumatic events, victims tend to try a number of strategies, including behavioral reenactment, in which the person acts either as a victim, with compulsive re-victimization by others, self-mutilation, or other self-destructive behavior or as a perpetrator, with violent, aggressive, or criminal behavior (van der Kolk, 1989). Another method, which is often very effective at obliterating the memories, but which frequently exacts a great cost, is the excessive or compulsive use of substances such as drugs or food. Self-mutilation and re-victimization might well be considered to be equivalent to substance use, because these behaviors activate endogenous opioid systems and can produce all the symptoms of drug addiction (van der Kolk, 1989).

The following clinical vignette illustrates the dissociative power and, therefore, the lure of drugs for victims of trauma:

> During a therapy session, one of Sharon's alternate personalities was reliving an episode in which she was serially raped by a group of sadistic men and women. Suddenly, her expression changed from one of terror and pain to one of relief and comfort. She explained to me that she was "floating." In other words, she had dissociated and left the body. (Some time later, another personality, who had occupied the body while the first one was dissociated, came out to relive that portion of the memory.) A few minutes after she began to dissociate, the first personality grew too tired to continue to float and returned to relive the remainder of the experience.
>
> During the next segment of the memory, one of the abusers gave Sharon an injection of a drug (unknown, but apparently a sedative), after which she began to look and behave similarly to how she looked and behaved while dissociated. I asked her if her feelings while drugged were anything like her feelings while floating. Smiling, she answered: "Yes. It feels just the same. But with the drugs, I don't have to work at it."

This story illustrates the fact that the subjective experience of being under the influence of drugs is very similar to the experience of dissociation. Drugs are capable of creating or augmenting dissociation.

Since drugs can mimic, create, or augment dissociation, it is likely that people who want or need to dissociate and who are aware of the power of drugs to help them accomplish it would develop a strong attachment to drugs. In other words, a person with a history of trauma, who has relied on dissociation as a defense to deal with that trauma, would seem to be very vulnerable to addiction. Therefore, it is possible, or likely, that high numbers of addicted persons also have PTSD or MPD.

Looking back, I realize that the dry drunk episodes I observed in chemical dependency treatment were probably intrusive recollections of early childhood trauma that were triggered by the treatment situation. It is likely that the dry drunks accompanied by memory gaps were caused by alternate personalities emerging to deal with the out-of-control memories. The transformations I observed were probably ego-states or alternate personalities being activated. Many relapses I witnessed were probably the result of failure to diagnose and treat a patient's PTSD or MPD or both. In fact, I recall so many events occurring in chemical dependency treatment that were probably indicative of dissociative experiences or disorders that I have concluded that addiction and dissociation are intimately linked and that any therapist who tries to help addicted patients should also be prepared to deal with dissociative disorders.

7

In Closing . . .

It seems appropriate to end this book with a few words of advice and encouragement for any readers who may be thinking of using Erickson-inspired therapeutic techniques with their chemically dependent patients. I'll address the first set of comments to those who have only recently begun to discover and explore Erickson and his style of therapy and who, though interested, may feel a bit unsure about being able to work the way Erickson did. These remarks will pick up and extend some of the ideas I introduced in Chapter 1. Then, I'll address those who are new to the field of chemical dependency treatment or are not involved in chemical dependency treatment as their primary focus. If you are new to *both* Erickson and chemical dependency, then I hope you find useful information in both sets of comments.

IF ERICKSON'S METHODS ARE NEW TO YOU

Now that you have been introduced to Milton Erickson and some of his methods, you are likely to have a mixture of feelings similar to the ones I had when I first encountered him: Excitement and enthusiasm to get underway, combined with a sense of being overwhelmed and mystified by the complexity of the kinds of things

Erickson was able to do. My thoughts at the time went something like this: "What a genius! I'd love to do what he does, but I have no idea how. It's really beyond me." I've written this book in hopes that it will get you off to a better start than I had, by trying to distill for you what it took me years of reading, thinking, and experimenting to learn, and present it to you in the simplest and clearest terms I could. Nevertheless, I would not be surprised if you still feel bewildered. That's why I want to give you a few pointers about how to *learn* to do Erickson-inspired therapy.

Please don't be dismayed if you aren't able, as the result of reading this book, to do therapy exactly the way Erickson would have done it. It is impossible for this or any book (or even all of them) about Erickson-inspired therapy techniques to prepare a therapist to work that way. "Book knowledge" alone cannot provide the necessary ingredients. You simply cannot master Erickson-inspired therapy techniques by mechanically memorizing and reproducing Erickson's (or any other therapist's, for that matter) words or mannerisms. That path will only lead you up a blind alley. Erickson understood this problem, and that is why he often cautioned students and followers against imitating him.

Key words that best characterize Erickson's style of therapy are *intuitive, creative, inspired, unconscious, strategic, flexible, responsive, complex, multileveled,* and other similar adjectives. These kinds of qualities cannot be learned by reading or observing alone, or by adopting them superficially, as one might try on an article of clothing. They must be developed on the inside, become a part of the therapist, and then emerge spontaneously, as if by fortunate accident. Am I saying that reading this book was a waste of time and money? Of course not. But if reading is not enough, what can a therapist do to learn to work in this new way?

First, alter your expectations. Realize that the learning curve is more gradual for Erickson-inspired therapy than for other modalities. It involves more than new behaviors. It involves an entirely new way of thinking. Allow time for this new way of thinking to sink in and take root. As you continue to expose yourself to more and different kinds of learnings, you will find yourself gradually changing and becoming increasingly capable of doing things in therapy that feel similar in spirit to the things that Erickson did.

Continue to read, and reread if necessary, everything you can get hold of that Erickson wrote or that pertains to Erickson and his approaches to therapy. Take in the information and stow it in the back of your mind. Don't try to force it to come together into a coherent whole. Allow it to come together on its own. If you encounter contradictions and confusion, accept these experiences as part of the learning process. They probably indicate that you are on the right track.

Attend conferences and workshops, and talk and listen to supervisors and colleagues who are familiar with Erickson. If consultants are available, utilize them. Although you should listen to and watch others carefully, don't try to model yourself too closely after anyone else. Simply take in the information and leave it alone. These people are just more sources of information to be put away and stored—much as you are advised to do with printed materials.

If you have not done so already, learn hypnosis. This training will teach you a completely different way of relating to patients, and the difference will be particularly striking to those who have a predominantly psychoanalytic or nondirective background. You will also learn a different way of thinking about how your patients or clients think and, more importantly, how they change. You will come to understand "trance logic"—that manner of reasoning in which contradictions don't matter, and rationality and intellect seem irrelevant. If you are fortunate enough to receive training that is thorough and extensive, you will be exposed to a number of different styles of using hypnosis, including Erickson's, and this will open up another channel for understanding how Erickson worked.

Start trying out new things in your daily therapeutic routine, just for the experience. Some of the new approaches you try may seem artificial, and it is possible that you will even worry (as I did) that you might start laughing in the middle and ruin it. Start (or continue) trusting your unconscious, and allow things to pop out of your mouth, even if these things seem unlike you. Be careful, though, since this looseness can occasionally backfire: You don't want to blurt out *everything* that runs through your mind, such as sexual fantasies you may be having about patients, or your anger, impatience, or boredom with them. Make sure that what wants to come out consists only of information or interventions designed to benefit the patient, and then let it out.

Strive to be completely *you* as a therapist, and only you. Don't try to be Erickson. He was better at that than anyone else ever has been or ever will be. But no one will ever be able to be you better than you can. From this standpoint, instead of struggling to be "Ericksonian," you can be an easier and more natural "You-ian."

Think of therapy more and more as a creative endeavor. Allow the creative impulse free rein. Let inspiration hit you from out of the blue. Go off on creative tangents. Conjure up metaphors to relate what you do in therapy to what other artists do in their art forms. For example, think of your work as if it were music, and consider the parts played by rhythm, pitch, harmony, pacing, and so on. Then, you might consider a therapy session as a mini-concert. Or paint pictures with words. Or think of yourself as an actor on a stage, as a dancer, or as a stand-up comic. Perhaps you can see similarities between doing group therapy and carving a sculpture. The possibilities are limitless.

Above all, have fun. See the humor in what you and your patients or clients do. Delight in the childlike qualities that shine through from inside both them and you. Catch and appreciate the absurdity and the irony of situations that arise in therapy, or of the entire premise of therapy itself. Stay loose, and let the therapy flow.

IF YOU ARE NEW TO CHEMICAL DEPENDENCY

I remember years ago meeting a new patient, an older man, who presented as very tense, agitated, and trembling. I suspected that he was having an anxiety attack and asked him a few questions, which he answered in a way that confirmed my diagnosis. I approached him as I had been trained to do, by trying relaxation training. Surprisingly, he did not respond, and instead suggested that I give him some medication. When I told him that I was not a physician and could not prescribe, he seemed upset and ended the interview early. Only later did I discover that the man was an alcoholic, that he had at the time been without a drink for a day and a half, and his "anxiety" was actually the symptoms of alcohol withdrawal. He was just "working" me to get a substance he needed, having mistaken me for a psychiatrist.

This experience is one of many that taught me that my standard mental health training not only failed to prepare me adequately to deal with chemically dependent people, but actually made it harder for me to learn than if I had had no previous training. If you are new to chemical dependency—even if you are a great therapist, even if you have mastered every nuance of Erickson-inspired therapy—please don't assume that you are ready to work with addicts and alcoholics. They are not "just another diagnostic group." They are different, and you will need an entirely new cognitive framework and set of skills to be able to help them.

Please recognize that you don't know enough yet. You can't. Then seek training. Work under the supervision of a seasoned chemical dependency veteran. Seek consultation. Attend A.A. meetings—lots of A.A. meetings. Read theoretical and clinical books, and read A.A. books and first-person accounts by people who have been through the experiences of addiction and recovery.

You are likely to encounter resistance from established chemical dependency programs or counselors. You are likely to encounter pockets of hostility toward mental health professionals. You are likely to be tested. You are likely to be made to feel like a buffoon or dismissed as if you were a child instead of a competent professional. You are likely to be made to feel like an outsider, as if you were a tourist who is welcome to visit as long as you keep your distance but never allowed to move in to stay. You are likely to encounter strongly held philosophical positions that are irrational but unshakable.

If these things happen to you, do not give up. They are part of your apprenticeship, and your apprenticeship will probably be tough. But hang in there, take your lumps, and keep learning. Eventually, you will arrive at a place where you think and behave differently, where your addicted patients rarely (you'll never see never) put things over on you, and where you receive the acceptance and respect of patients, colleagues in the field, and the recovering community.

LET'S MARCH TOGETHER

I am aware that I may be portraying both Erickson-inspired therapy and chemical dependency treatment in ways that make them seem tough—certainly not for the faint of heart. Well, that's appropriate, because that's how I see them. But don't be scared away. Stay around and join the small but growing army of Erickson-inspired chemical dependency clinicians. We will join forces to combat a terrible foe, the disease of addiction. And along the way our creative faculties will be stretched as we call on our innermost resources to face the many unexpected and difficult challenges we are sure to encounter. Each day, we will grow wiser and better at what we do. We will stick together and cheer each other on. And we will delight in the incredibly beautiful scenery of the terrain that we will cover as we keep marching along.

BIBLIOGRAPHY

Alcoholics Anonymous. (1957). *Alcoholics Anonymous Comes of Age*. New York: Alcoholics Anonymous World Services, Inc.

Alcoholics Anonymous. (1976). *Alcoholics Anonymous*. New York: Alcoholics Anonymous World Services, Inc.

Alcoholics Anonymous. (1988). *Twelve Steps and Twelve Traditions*. New York: Alcoholics Anonymous World Services, Inc.

American Psychiatric Association. (1987). *Diagnostic and Statistical Manual of Mental Disorders* (3rd ed., rev.). Washington, D.C.: American Psychiatric Association.

Bandler, R., & Grinder, J. (1975). *Patterns of the Hypnotic Technique of Milton H. Erickson, M.D.* (Vol. 1). Cupertino, CA: Meta Publications.

Bateson, G. (1971). The cybernetics of "self": A theory of alcoholism. *Psychiatry, 34*, 1–18.

Bliss, E.L. (1984). Spontaneous self-hypnosis in multiple personality disorder. *Psychiatric Clinics of North America, 7*, 135–149.

Braun, B.G. (Ed.). (1986). *Treatment of Multiple Personality Disorder*. Washington, D.C.: American Psychiatric Press.

Coons, P.M. (1984). The differential diagnosis of multiple personality: A comprehensive review. *Psychiatric Clinics of North America, 7*, 51–67.

Cutter, F. (1975, April). *Problem solving roles as alcoholism treatment*. Paper presented at the Meeting of the Western Psychological Association, Sacramento, California.

Erickson, M.H. (1967a). Further techniques of hypnosis—

Utilization techniques. In J. Haley (Ed.), *Advanced Techniques of Hypnosis and Therapy* (pp. 32–50). New York: Grune & Stratton.

Erickson, M.H. (1967b). The "surprise" and "my-friend-John" techniques of hypnosis: Minimal cues and natural field experimentation. In J. Haley (Ed.), *Advanced Techniques of Hypnosis and Therapy* (pp. 101–117). New York: Grune & Stratton.

Erickson, M.H. (1967c). The confusion technique in hypnosis. In J. Haley (Ed.), *Advanced Techniques of Hypnosis and Therapy* (pp. 130–157). New York: Grune & Stratton.

Erickson, M.H. (1967d). Indirect hypnotherapy of an enuretic couple. In J. Haley (Ed.), *Advanced Techniques of Hypnosis and Therapy* (pp. 410–412). New York: Grune & Stratton.

Erickson, M.H. (1977). Hypnotic approaches to therapy. *American Journal of Clinical Hypnosis, 20,* 20–35.

Erickson, M.H., & Rossi, E.L. (1979). *Hypnotherapy: An Exploratory Casebook.* New York: Irvington.

Erickson, M.H., Rossi, E.L., & Rossi, S.I. (1976). *Hypnotic Realities.* New York: Irvington.

Franklin, B. (1968). *The Autobiography of Benjamin Franklin.* New York: Lancer.

Haley, J. (1963). *Strategies of Psychotherapy.* New York: Grune & Stratton.

Haley, J. (Ed.). (1967). *Advanced Techniques of Hypnosis and Therapy.* New York: Grune & Stratton.

Haley, J. (1973). *Uncommon Therapy.* New York: Norton.

Haley, J. (1984). *Ordeal Therapy.* San Francisco: Jossey-Bass.

Haley, J. (Ed.). (1985). *Conversations with Milton H. Erickson, M.D.* (Vol. 1, Changing Individuals). New York: Triangle Press.

Horevitz, R.P., & Braun, B.G. (1984). Are multiple personalities borderline? An analysis of 33 cases. *Psychiatric Clinics of North America, 7,* 69–87.

Horn, D.L., & Lovern, J.D. (1981, February). *Evoking the "hated self" in the treatment of alcoholics.* Paper presented at the meeting of the California State Psychological Association, Sacramento, California.

Jacobs, D.F. (1987). Evidence for a common dissociative-like reaction among addicts. *Journal of Gambling Behavior, 4,* 27–37.

James, W. (1958). *The Varieties of Religious Experience.* New York: New American Library.

Johnson, C., & Connors, M.E. (1987). *The Etiology and Treatment of Bulimia Nervosa.* New York: Basic Books.

Johnson, V.E. (1980). *I'll Quit Tomorrow.* New York: Harper & Row.

Jung, C.G. (1968). *Analytical Psychology: Its Theory and Practice.* New York: Vintage Books.

Kluft, R.P. (1987a). An update on multiple personality disorder. *Hospital and Community Psychiatry, 38,* 363–373.

Kluft, R.P. (Ed.). (1987b). *Childhood Antecedents of Multiple Personality.* Washington, D.C.: American Psychiatric Press.

Kuley, N.B., & Jacobs, D.F. (1988). The relationship between dissociative-like experiences and sensation seeking among social and problem gamblers. *Journal of Gambling Behavior, 4,* 197–207.

Lovern, J.D. (1980). Indirect hypnotic communication as a group therapy technique in alcoholism treatment. In H. Wain (Ed.), *Clinical Hypnosis in Medicine* (pp. 173–191). Chicago: Yearbook Medical Publishers.

Lovern, J.D. (1981, November-December). Starting at the bottom. *Alcoholism/The National Magazine,* 28–30.

Lovern, J.D. (1985). Unconscious factors in recovery from alcoholism. In J. Zeig (Ed.), *Ericksonian Psychotherapy.* (Vol. 2, Clinical Applications). (pp. 373–383). New York: Brunner/Mazel.

Lovern, J.D. (1990, April). *Food, drugs, and dissociation: Breaking the addictive cycle in multiple personality disorder.* Paper presented at the Third Annual Orange County Confence on Multiple Personality and Dissociation, Newport Beach, CA.

Lovern, J.D., & Zohn, J. (1982). Utilization and indirect suggestion in multiple-family group therapy with alcoholics. *Journal of Marital and Family Therapy, 8,* 325–333.

Narcotics Anonymous. (1987). *Narcotics Anonymous.* Van Nuys, CA: Narcotics Anonymous World Service Office, Inc.

Overeaters Anonymous, (1980). *Overeaters Anonymous.* Torrance, CA: Overeaters Anonymous, Inc.

Rioch, M.J. (1970). The work of Wilfred Bion on groups. *Psychiatry, 33,* 56–66.

Royce, J.E. (1981). *Alcohol Problems and Alcoholism: A Comprehensive Survey.* New York: Free Press.

Ryan, C., & Butters, N. (1986). The neuropsychology of alcoholism. In D. Wedding, A.M. Horton, & J. Webster (Eds.), *The Neuropsychology Handbook* (pp. 376–409). New York: Springer.

Sanders, S. (1986). The perceptual alteration scale: A scale measuring dissociation. *American Journal of Clinical Hypnosis, 29,* 95–102.

Solomon, R.L. (1980). The opponent-process theory of acquired motivation. *American Psychologist, 35,* 691–712.

Solomon, R.L., & Corbit, J.D. (1974). An opponent-process theory of motivation: I. Temporal dynamics of affect. *Psychology Review, 81,* 119–145.

Spiegel, D. (1984). Multiple personality as a post-traumatic stress disorder. *Psychiatric Clinics of North America, 7,* 101–110.

Spiegel, D. (1986). Dissociating damage. *American Journal of Clinical Hypnosis, 29,* 123–131.

Stern, C.R. (1984). The etiology of multiple personalities. *Psychiatric Clinics of North America, 7,* 149–159.

Thomsen, R. (1975). *Bill W.* New York: Popular Library.

Tiebout, H.M. (1942). Private hospital and the care of alcoholic patients. *Diseases of the Nervous System, 3,* 202–205.

Tiebout, H.M. (1944). Therapeutic mechanisms of Alcoholics Anonymous. *American Journal of Psychiatry, 100,* 468–473.

Tiebout, H.M. (1945). Syndrome of alcohol addiction. *Quarterly Journal of Studies on Alcohol, 5,* 535–546.

Tiebout, H.M. (1946). Psychology and the treatment of alcoholism. *Quarterly Journal of Studies on Alcohol, 7,* 214–227.

Tiebout, H.M. (1947). The problem of gaining cooperation from the alcoholic patient. *Quarterly Journal of Studies on Alcohol, 8,* 47–54.

Tiebout, H.M. (1948). Alcoholism: Its nature and treatment. *Medical Clinics of North America, 32*, 687–693.

Tiebout, H.M. (1949). The act of surrender in the therapeutic process. *Quarterly Journal of Studies on Alcohol, 10*, 48– 58.

Tiebout, H.M. (1951). The role of psychiatry in the field of alcoholism. *Quarterly Journal of Studies on Alcohol, 12*, 52–57.

Tiebout, H.M. (1953). Surender versus compliance in therapy with special reference to alcoholism. *Quarterly Journal of Studies on Alcohol, 14*, 58–68.

Tiebout, H.M. (1954). The ego factors in recovery from alcoholism. *Quarterly Journal of Studies on Alcohol, 15*, 610–621.

Tiebout, H.M. (1962). Intervention in psychotherapy. *American Journal of Psychoanalysis, 22*, 74–80.

Torem, M.S. (1986). Dissociative states presenting as an eating disorder. *American Journal of Clinical Hypnosis, 29*, 137–142.

Torem, M.S. (1987). Ego-State therapy for eating disorders. *American Journal of Clinical Hypnosis, 30*, 94–103.

United States Department of Health, Education, and Welfare, NIAAA. (1974). *Alcohol and Health: Second Special Report to the United States Congress.* Washington, D.C.: U.S. Government Printing Office.

van der Kolk, B.A. (1989). The compulsion to repeat the trauma: Re-enactment, revictimization, and masochism. *Psychiatric Clinics of North America, 12*, 389–411.

W., L.B. (1979). *Lois remembers.* New York: Al-Anon Family Group Headquarters, Inc.

Watkins, H.H. (1984). Ego-state theory and therapy. In J. Corsini (Ed.), *Encyclopedia of Psychology* (Vol. 1). New York: Wiley.

Watkins, J.G., & Johnson, R.J. (1982). *We, the Divided Self.* New York: Irvington.

Wegscheider, S. (1981). *Another Chance: Hope and Health for the Alcoholic Family.* Palo Alto, CA: Science and Behavior Books.

Whitaker, D.S., & Lieberman, M.A. (1964). *Psychotherapy through the Group Process.* Chicago: Aldine.

Yalom, I.D. 1975). *The Theory and Practice of Group Psychotherapy.* New York: Basic Books.

INDEX

223